# in the mood for
# entertaining

# JO PRATT

# in the mood for
# entertaining

## DELICIOUS FOOD FOR ALL OCCASIONS

*Photography by* Gareth Morgans
*Illustrations by* Cecilia Carlstedt

MICHAEL JOSEPH
*an imprint of*
PENGUIN BOOKS

# FOR ALL MY FRIENDS AND FAMILY

MICHAEL JOSEPH

Published by the Penguin Group

Penguin Books Ltd, 80 Strand, London WC2R 0RL, England

Penguin Group (USA) Inc., 375 Hudson Street, New York, New York 10014, USA

Penguin Group (Canada), 90 Eglinton Avenue East, Suite 700, Toronto, Ontario, Canada M4P 2Y3 (a division of Pearson Penguin Canada Inc.)

Penguin Ireland, 25 St Stephen's Green, Dublin 2, Ireland (a division of Penguin Books Ltd)

Penguin Group (Australia), 250 Camberwell Road, Camberwell, Victoria 3124, Australia (a division of Pearson Australia Group Pty Ltd)

Penguin Books India Pvt Ltd, 11 Community Centre, Panchsheel Park, New Delhi – 110 017, India

Penguin Group (NZ), 67 Apollo Drive, Rosedale, North Shore 0632, New Zealand (a division of Pearson New Zealand Ltd)

Penguin Books (South Africa) (Pty) Ltd, 24 Sturdee Avenue, Rosebank, Johannesburg 2196, South Africa

Penguin Books Ltd, Registered Offices: 80 Strand, London WC2R 0RL, England

www.penguin.com

First published 2009

1

Copyright © Jo Pratt, 2009

Photography copyright © Gareth Morgans, 2009

Illustrations copyright © Cecilia Carlstedt, 2009

Prop styling by Wei Tang

The moral right of the author has been asserted

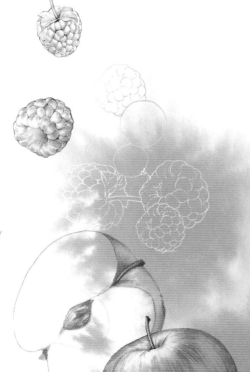

Set in Bodoni and Helvetica

Printed in Singapore

A CIP catalogue record for this book is available from the British Library

ISBN: 978–0–718–15406–6

# INTRODUCTION

*Blimey, where do I start? It's been about two and a half years since my last book,* In the Mood for Food, *hit the shelves and in that time I've had a little boy (hi, Olly), moved house, moved out of house while nice things are done to it and moved back in. I've also been hard at it writing this book, the 'difficult second album'.*

*For those of you who don't know me, I'm Jo Pratt, a home cook who has been making up recipes for as long as I can remember. (I used to dye mashed potato and wrap it in lettuce leaves – urrggh!) Over the years I have been fortunate enough to work with the best chefs in the business, write for magazines including* Glamour *and* Olive, *appear on TV and write, as I've mentioned, a cookbook that was fantastically well received.* In the Mood for Food *has been a huge success for me and it has opened up many doors, including the opportunity to write this book.*

*So, what's this new book's big idea, I hear you say? Well, it's all about entertaining. Continuing on with the idea of moods, in this book you'll find recipes for every entertaining occasion. So if you're in the mood for a good gossip with your best mate, then the recipes for fancy cakes to take (or scoff) with tea during the afternoon are a must or if you're in a house party mood, how does a Moroccan-themed menu sound? I'll leave the fancy dress ideas to you, but do please send pictures.*

*All the recipes are stylish, fuss-free and easy to follow and you'll find culinary hints and tips, presentation ideas and even drinks suggestions. The book is split into four chapters, which are as follows:*

'ALL THE RECIPES ARE STYLISH, FUSS-FREE AND EASY TO FOLLOW AND YOU'LL FIND CULINARY HINTS AND TIPS, PRESENTATION IDEAS AND EVEN DRINK SUGGESTIONS.'

TWO'S COMPANY *As you'll see, this chapter is all about entertaining for two. There's Midweek Masterpieces for when beans on toast don't quite send out the right vibes and you'll also find a whole sweet trolley of cakes and cookies for impressing your mother-in-law, gran or, as mentioned, your best mate. There are two three-course menus for special Saturday nights in and if, for example, it's your other half's birthday, then they're going to love being entertained in bed with Ricotta and Coconut Hotcakes with Espresso Syrup.*

RELAXED ENTERTAINING *You're in the mood for a night in with friends or family and a takeaway pizza or rotisserie chicken from the local supermarket is not going to hit the spot. So, there are sparkly cocktails and Cappuccino Knickerbocker Glories (what else?) for girly nights in and Hot and Spicy Nuts and steaks for when you boys have a cards night (or whatever else you do when you have an evening in together). Seasonal Friday night suppers and a variety of Sunday lunches, from the slightly different to the quick and easy, also feature in this chapter.*

THE 'DINNER PARTY' *I can hear those words now. You're having a dinner party and the doorbell goes, announcing the arrival of your first guests – 'OH, SHOOT! THEY'RE HERE! WE'RE NOT READY!' This chapter is all about satisfying you when you're in the mood to have a dinner party, while trying to make the organization and the 'what to cook?' part a little less hassle. Dress up, get your best plates out and take your pick from these great menus, where each course (from three right up to seven) complements the other. There's even a section called Pimp Up Your Dinner Party (do you think MTV will be interested?).*

FEEDING A CROWD *Over the last couple of years, my parents and my husband's parents have celebrated 'milestone birthdays' (see, Mum – your age is still a secret), we've christened our new house and our little boy and seem to have been involved with lots of other large get-togethers, from wedding celebrations to first birthdays (it must be my age). Anyway, from my experience parties for a large amount of people are not easy things to do when you don't have staff. This chapter is all about food for such occasions and hopefully the recipes should make things a little easier when planning how to feed your crowd. Unfortunately there aren't any tips for making the washing-up go away.*

*That's it, four chapters of delicious recipes that will hopefully be a big help when the mood to entertain springs up. I hope your friends and family enjoy the recipes as much as my friends and family have (or so they tell me!).*

*Enjoy.*

Jo x

# CHAPTER ONE
# TWO'S COMPANY

A chapter for all those times you're in the mood for entertaining just that one special person. There's nothing better than being treated to a breakfast fit for a king and my breakfasts and brunches for lovers are certainly regal. I also know that serving my husband Sweet Potato Hash Browns with Sausages and Sweet Chilli Tomatoes on a Sunday morning will put a few credits in the bank – it's so true that the way to a man's heart is through his stomach.

Midweek masterpieces are about making Tuesdays, Wednesdays and Thursdays the new Fridays. Do you always meet your best mate in a bar or restaurant? Why not mix it up a bit and get them round to Chez Vous? In this section you'll find a range of dishes that are simple to put together and use ingredients that are readily available. What's the worst that can happen – you save a few quid?

There are also two special three-course menus here for romantic weekend nights in, which go perfectly with candles and Barry White. Cook together with your partner and a glass of wine or two and you'll have no bill at the end of the night and no cab home – sounds like the perfect Saturday evening to me.

Lastly, Tea for Two is all about afternoon teas for your family and best friends. Drizzle, kisses, chocolate, cookies, cake, tarts, macaroons, Swiss roll – you get the picture? This is a whole section for the sweet teeth of you and your best mate. Get your gossip radar working and the kettle on.

So, how's that for a first chapter? Can it get any better? Oh yes, it can . . .

# BREAKFAST AND BRUNCH

*Forget nipping into town to get a load of croissants or making a fried egg sarnie, spend a bit of time making your first meal of the weekend special – just don't get Espresso Syrup on the bed sheets.*

# Menu

*Maple, Pecan and Sultana Pastry Twirls*

*Ricotta and Coconut Hotcakes*
  *with Espresso Syrup*

*Cherry, Pistachio and Honey Granola*

*Smoked Salmon and Cream Cheese Omelette*

*Grilled Tomatoes and Melting Brie on Sourdough*

*Sweet Potato Hash Browns*
  *with Sausages and Sweet Chilli Tomatoes*

# MAPLE, PECAN AND SULTANA PASTRY TWIRLS

There's really only one thing that beats having pastries in the morning, and that's making them yourself.

• **MAKES 10**   • **40 MINUTES**

375g ready-rolled puff pastry
100g pecan nuts, chopped
100g sultanas
8 tablespoons maple syrup
2 teaspoons ground cinnamon
1 egg, beaten
1½ tablespoons demerara sugar

Preheat the oven to 200°C/fan 180°C/gas 6. Line ten holes of a twelve-hole bun or muffin tin with 10–12cm square pieces of baking paper or non-stick paper muffin cases.

Cut the pastry widthways into ten strips, which will be approximately 3cm wide.

Mix together the pecan nuts, sultanas, maple syrup and cinnamon. Spoon on top of the pasty strips and spread lightly. Roll each strip of pastry to form a coil and sit in the bun or muffin tin. Brush the top of the pastry and any edges you can see with the beaten egg and scatter the demerara sugar over the top.

Bake in the oven for 20 to 25 minutes until golden brown. Serve warm.

**PS . . .** To make Maple, Pecan and Chocolate Pastry Twirls, swap the sultanas for 100g dark or milk chocolate drops and use the grated zest of 1 orange instead of the ground cinnamon. Why not make half the quantity of each so you get the choice of both flavours for brunch?

# RICOTTA AND COCONUT HOTCAKES WITH ESPRESSO SYRUP

I think one of my best-loved breakfast recipes is pancakes, or hotcakes. You can experiment with all sorts of flavour combinations, but these are my current favourite as they're lovely and light to eat, but still seem to keep me satisfied for hours.

• MAKES 10 TO 12 HOTCAKES   • 30 MINUTES

*for the syrup*
300ml espresso coffee
150g caster sugar

*for the hotcakes*
125g ricotta cheese
150ml coconut milk
2 eggs, separated
150g plain flour
1 teaspoon baking powder
50g desiccated coconut
2 tablespoons caster sugar
sea salt
vegetable oil

sliced banana, pineapple,
    mango or other fresh
    fruit of your choice
    (if you fancy it), to serve

To make the espresso syrup, place the espresso and sugar in a saucepan, bring to the boil and cook until the liquid has reduced by half. Leave to cool and, as it cools, it will take on a syrupy consistency.

For the pancakes, mix together the ricotta, coconut milk and egg yolks. Sift over the flour and add the baking powder, desiccated coconut, caster sugar and a pinch of salt and mix until everything is just combined (if you overmix then you won't have such light hotcakes).

In a separate bowl, whisk the egg whites until they form stiff peaks. Add a spoonful to the ricotta mixture to loosen and then fold in the rest with a large metal spoon, trying not to knock out all of the air from the whites.

Heat a large non-stick frying or pancake pan with a little oil. Drop a few spoonfuls of the batter into the pan, leaving enough space between each to turn them. Cook over a low to medium heat for a couple of minutes until golden underneath (lift an edge to have a peek). Flip over using a palette knife or fish slice and cook for a further minute or so until golden. Keep warm (on a plate with a tea towel over the top near the hob or in a low oven) while you continue to cook the rest, adding a little more oil to the pan for each batch.

Serve the pancakes with the syrup drizzled all over and some fresh fruit on the side (if you fancy it).

# CHERRY, PISTACHIO AND HONEY GRANOLA

If, like me, you're not a fan of dusty muesli that looks, and quite often tastes, like sawdust, then you'll love this granola. It's fruity, chunky, crunchy, nutty and delicious served with ice-cold milk or yoghurt. If you want to be a little more fancy when serving it, try my PS . . . suggestion below.

• **MAKES 8 TO 10 PORTIONS**   • **40 TO 50 MINUTES**

175g runny honey
100g unsalted butter
225g rolled oats
100g barley or rye flakes
100g flaked almonds
100g pumpkin seeds
    or sunflower seeds
    (or a combination of both)
25g unsweetened
    desiccated coconut
200g dried cherries,
    roughly chopped if large
125g pistachio nuts,
    roughly chopped
milk or yoghurt, to serve

Preheat the oven to 160°C/fan 140°C/gas 2–3.

Place the honey and butter in a large saucepan over a low heat and stir until the butter has melted. Remove from the heat and stir in the oats, barley or rye, flaked almonds, pumpkin or sunflower seeds and coconut. Spread evenly on to a large non-stick baking tray (or one lined with baking paper) and bake for 30 to 40 minutes until crunchy and golden, mixing around a couple of times for even cooking.

Leave to cool completely and transfer to a bowl. Stir in the cherries and pistachios. Serve either straight away with the milk or yoghurt or store in an airtight container for up to 1 month.

**PS . . .** Mix a portion of the granola with a good glug of apple, pomegranate or cranberry juice. Layer in a serving dish or tall glass with some Greek yoghurt and your choice of fresh fruit, such as kiwi, mango, summer berries, pineapple, peaches/nectarines, banana and pomegranate seeds. Serve straight away.

# SMOKED SALMON AND CREAM CHEESE OMELETTE

This is a rather posh version of a traditional omelette. Serve with some fresh juice, perhaps in a champagne glass. In fact, why not make it a buck's fizz?

• SERVES 2  • 15 MINUTES

6 eggs
2 tablespoons chopped chives
100g smoked salmon, cut into pieces
freshly ground black pepper
25g butter
100g cream cheese

It's much easier to make one omelette at a time in a small frying pan. They are really quick to make, so it's still possible to serve them at the same time. Just keep the first one warm in a low oven while you make the second one.

So, to make one omelette, break three of the eggs into a bowl and whisk together with a fork. Stir in the half of the chives, half the smoked salmon and a twist of pepper.

Warm a small (approximately 15cm) non-stick omelette pan over a medium heat. Add half of the butter and swirl around to coat the base and sides. Once the butter is starting to foam, add the egg mixture and move around in the pan with the base of a fork (taking care not to scratch your pan) until you have a soft scrambled consistency. Now leave the omelette to finish cooking so the egg is just set. This should only take a minute or so.

Soften the cream cheese with a spoon and spread or spoon half of it on to one side of the omelette. Fold the other half of the omelette over the top and tip on to a plate. Keep warm while you repeat the process with the remaining ingredients.

Serve the omelettes as they are or with some crusty buttered toast.

**PS . . .** Try chopped ham, salami, cooked prawns, sautéed mushrooms or a little grated courgette instead of the salmon. Other herbs such as basil, parsley, tarragon and dill can also be used. Cottage cheese, ricotta, mascarpone and grated cheeses are all good instead of the cream cheese.

# GRILLED TOMATOES AND MELTING BRIE ON SOURDOUGH

Cheese on toast for breakfast? Somehow this works. It's lovely, and great if you've overdone it the night before.

• SERVES 2   • 25 MINUTES

6 medium-sized tomatoes
3 tablespoons olive oil
1 clove of garlic, crushed
1 teaspoon dried oregano
sea salt and freshly ground
  black pepper
4 slices of sourdough bread
100–125g Brie, thinly sliced

Preheat the grill to high.

Cut the tomatoes in half and sit them on a piece of foil on one side of a large baking tray.

In a small bowl, mix together the olive oil, garlic, oregano and a good pinch of salt and freshly ground black pepper. Spoon the flavoured oil on top of the tomatoes and over one side of the sourdough slices.

Place the tomatoes under the grill and cook for about 8 minutes, then add the sourdough to the other side of the baking tray and grill for about 3 minutes each side until golden. By now the tomatoes should be cooked and just holding their shape.

Remove the tray from the grill. Sit the tomatoes on top of the toasted sourdough and pour over any juices collected in the foil. Lay the sliced Brie over the top and return the tray back under the grill for a few minutes until melted.

Transfer to plates and serve straight away.

# SWEET POTATO HASH BROWNS WITH SAUSAGES AND SWEET CHILLI TOMATOES

As I mentioned in the introduction to this chapter, this will certainly gain you credits if you serve it to your partner on a Saturday or Sunday morning.

• SERVES 2   • 20 MINUTES

2–3 tablespoons olive oil

4–6 sausages (whatever type/flavour you fancy)

150g sweet potato (peeled weight)

1 egg

sea salt and freshly ground black pepper

200g cherry tomatoes

1 teaspoon caster sugar

1 teaspoon balsamic vinegar

a pinch of dried chilli flakes

flat-leaf parsley to garnish

Heat 1 tablespoon of the olive oil in a medium to large non-stick frying pan. Cut the sausages into 1–2cm thick slices on an angle with a sharp knife, add to the frying pan and fry for roughly 5 minutes until cooked through and just becoming golden. Once cooked, remove from the pan and keep warm.

Grate the sweet potato using the coarse part of the grater. Place in a bowl, mix in the egg and season with the salt and pepper. Divide into four.

If there isn't much oil in the pan, add a tablespoon more. Once hot, place the mixture in the pan, flatten each hash brown slightly with a spoon and cook for 2 to 3 minutes each side or until golden and crispy.

While the hash browns are cooking, heat the remaining tablespoon of oil in a separate small frying pan. Add the tomatoes and cook until they are beginning to soften. Add the caster sugar, balsamic vinegar and chilli flakes and season with salt and pepper. Cook for a couple of minutes so the tomatoes are all squishy.

Serve two hash browns each, topped with the sausages and tomatoes. Add a piece of flat-leaf parsley on each plate for a nice bit of colour.

**PS . . .** For a more 'sophisticated' alternative to the sausages and tomatoes, top the hash browns with cooked asparagus, poached eggs and some crème fraîche mixed with chives and lemon juice.

# MIDWEEK MASTERPIECES

*Getting together with your best friend in the week is a great idea. It means you have fewer people to catch up with at the weekend, and they might bring wine and flowers as a thank-you – bonus.*

# Menu

## Savoury

Blue Cheese Macaroni Gratin

Roast Garlic and Olive Tagliatelle
  with Ricotta

Crispy Tarragon Chicken
  with Butter Bean, Leek and Mustard Mash

Harissa and Lemon Salmon
  with Minted Bulgur Salad

Maple-glazed Gammon
  with Chilli Pineapple Salsa and Crunchy Potatoes

## Sweet

Cinnamon and Raisin Rice Pudding
  with Caramelized Apples

Baked Plums
  with Port and Orange Mascarpone

Tipsy Oranges
  with Vanilla Cream

Mocha Toffee Sundaes

Raspberry and Elderflower Syllabub

# BLUE CHEESE MACARONI GRATIN

For a chilly evening you can't beat this comforting, grown-up version of macaroni cheese. The tangy blue cheese and white wine in the sauce prevent it from being too stodgy or rich (and that means a dessert should definitely follow).

• SERVES 2  • 25 MINUTES

250g macaroni

20g butter

1 bunch of spring onions, thinly sliced

1 sprig of thyme

20g plain flour

200ml white wine

125ml single cream

150g blue cheese, such as Cashel Blue, Gorgonzola, Danish Blue or Stilton

sea salt and freshly ground black pepper

1 roasted red pepper (from a jar), cut into strips

2 large handfuls of baby spinach leaves

olive oil, for drizzling

Start off by cooking the macaroni until tender.

While the pasta is cooking, melt the butter in a saucepan and add the spring onions and sprig of thyme. Cook for a couple of minutes until the spring onions are softened. Stir in the flour and cook for a minute or so, stirring most of the time so the flour doesn't burn.

Gradually pour in the white wine, stirring continuously. Add the cream and bring to a simmer. Cook for about 5 minutes to thicken slightly. Remove the sprig of thyme.

Thinly slice half of the blue cheese and keep to one side. Crumble, break or chop the rest and stir into the sauce. Season with just a pinch of salt as the blue cheese is naturally salty and add a good twist of black pepper. Cook until the cheese has melted.

Drain the macaroni well and mix into the sauce. Finally, stir in the red pepper and spinach leaves. Spoon the mixture into two individual shallow gratin dishes or one larger one to share. Lay the sliced blue cheese on top, add a twist of black pepper and drizzle over the surface with some olive oil.

Heat your grill to its highest setting. Place the dish or dishes on a baking sheet and grill for just about 5 minutes until the top is lightly golden and bubbling. Serve straight away just as it is or with a nice green salad.

**PS . . .** If you wanted to make this ahead of time, place the dish/dishes in the fridge and when you're ready to eat, bake in the oven (180°C/fan 160°C/gas 4) for about 30 to 40 minutes, or until golden and bubbling.

# ROAST GARLIC AND OLIVE TAGLIATELLE WITH RICOTTA

It's well worth keeping your kitchen stocked with these ingredients, then you can throw this dish together at short notice. It's really easy to prepare and the smell of roasting garlic is just fantastic.

• SERVES 2   • 30 MINUTES

200–300g tagliatelle

6 plump cloves of garlic, left whole

100g stoned black olives, such as Greek kalamata

2 tablespoons extra-virgin olive oil, plus extra for drizzling

40g pine nuts

a handful of oregano leaves

grated zest and juice of ½ lemon

sea salt and freshly ground black pepper

150g ricotta cheese

Preheat the oven to 200°C/fan 180°C/gas 6.

Depending on the type of pasta you are using, the cooking times will differ, but you just need to cook the tagliatelle so that it is ready at the same time as the roasted sauce. I like to use a rich egg pasta that only takes 3 to 4 minutes to cook, but the type you use is up to you. Cook the pasta until al dente.

Place the garlic and olives in a small roasting tray or cake tin and toss in the olive oil. Roast in the oven for 20 minutes, turning them occasionally to ensure even cooking.

Add the pine nuts to the garlic and olives, coating them in the oil, and then return to the oven for 5 minutes. Stir in the oregano leaves and roast for a final 3 minutes. This is just long enough for the oregano to crisp up slightly, releasing all of its lovely flavour.

Drain the pasta, reserving about 100ml of the cooking water in the bottom of the pan. Return the pasta to the pan, place back on the heat and toss with the lemon zest and juice. Tip all of the roasted goodies into the pasta pan along with a pinch of salt and a good twist of black pepper and stir around to mix. You can add the ricotta to the pan at this stage and stir in or add it afterwards.

Spoon into pasta bowls and, if you haven't already added it, place little spoonfuls of ricotta on top of the pasta. Add a twist of pepper, a drizzle of olive oil and serve straight away.

**PS . . .** Torn pieces of buffalo mozzarella and even a soft curd cheese are tasty alternatives to the ricotta.

# CRISPY TARRAGON CHICKEN
# WITH BUTTER BEAN, LEEK AND MUSTARD MASH

This is a great recipe to serve at any time of the year. The chicken breasts are flavoured with a tarragon paste (similar to a pesto), which can easily be made a day or two ahead of time. If preferred, basil or chives could also be used. As for the mash – it's so easy to make and tastes delicious.

• SERVES 2   • 30 MINUTES

### for the chicken

15g bunch of tarragon, roughly chopped

10g bunch of flat-leaf parsley, roughly chopped

25g pine nuts, lightly toasted

15g Parmesan cheese, finely grated

finely grated zest of 1 lemon

1 clove of garlic, crushed

5 tablespoons (75ml) extra-virgin olive oil

sea salt and freshly ground black pepper

2 boneless chicken breasts, skin on

1 tablespoon olive oil

### for the mash

25g butter

1 medium leek

400g can of butter beans, drained

100ml chicken stock

1 teaspoon wholegrain mustard

sea salt and freshly ground black pepper

steamed green vegetables, such as mangetout, sugar snap peas, asparagus tips, tenderstem broccoli or green beans, to serve

To prepare the chicken, place the tarragon, parsley, pine nuts, Parmesan, lemon zest, garlic, extra-virgin olive oil and seasoning in a food processor and whizz until you have a relatively smooth paste/pesto consistency.

Place the chicken breasts on a board and gently push your finger between the skin and the flesh to form a pocket. Place about a tablespoon of the 'pesto' inside each pocket and gently press around to cover the surface.

Heat the tablespoon of olive oil in a large heavy-based frying pan over a low to medium heat. Season the chicken skin with sea salt and then place, skin-side down, in the pan. Cook gently, without turning or moving around too much, for 8 to 10 minutes until the skin is wonderfully golden and crispy. Turn over and cook for a further few minutes or until cooked though. Once cooked, remove from the pan and leave to rest for a couple of minutes.

While the chicken is cooking, melt the butter in a saucepan. Cut the leek in half lengthways and fairly thinly slice. Cook the leek for a few minutes in the butter until it is softened, but not coloured. Add the butter beans, stock and mustard and cook for 2 to 3 minutes until the butter beans are piping hot. Using a potato masher, mash to give you a chunky texture. Season with salt and pepper.

Serve the chicken, mash and vegetables of your choice with the extra tarragon pesto on the side or save it to use in the same way another day. It will keep in the fridge for a few days.

# HARISSA AND LEMON SALMON WITH MINTED BULGUR SALAD

For a summer's evening this is perfect because you can prepare everything an hour or so ahead of time and then sit outside with a nice cold drink before finishing off the salmon just before serving. I'll often double up on the Minted Bulgur Salad and enjoy it the next day with some feta cheese crumbled into it.

• SERVES 2   • 20 MINUTES, PLUS UP TO 1 HOUR MARINATING

*for the salmon*

2 teaspoons harissa paste

grated zest and juice
    of ½ lemon

2 tablespoons Greek yoghurt

sea salt and freshly ground
    black pepper

2 salmon fillets, skin on

a drop of olive oil

*for the salad*

150g bulgur wheat

250ml very hot chicken or
    vegetable stock

approximately 10g mint
    leaves, finely chopped

10cm piece of cucumber,
    finely diced

4 spring onions, finely chopped

1 stick of celery, thinly sliced

seeds from ½ pomegranate
    (optional)

juice of ½ lemon

2 tablespoons extra-virgin
    olive oil

To prepare the salmon, mix together the harissa, lemon zest and juice, yoghurt and seasoning in a shallow bowl. Coat the salmon and leave in the fridge to marinate for up to 1 hour, depending on how long you have.

While the salmon is in the marinade, you can prepare the salad. Place the bulgur wheat in a bowl and pour over the hot stock. Stir, cover with clingfilm and leave for the bulgur wheat to absorb the liquid and cool down. This will take about 15 minutes. Alternatively, you can follow the cooking instructions on the back of the packet.

Stir the remaining salad ingredients into the bulgur wheat and the salad is ready.

To cook the salmon, heat a griddle or frying pan until it is really hot, add the drop of oil and cook the salmon for 5 to 7 minutes, depending on the thickness of the fish, turning halfway through. It is best to cook the fish skin-side up to start with.

Divide the minted bulgur salad between two plates and sit the salmon on the side.

**PS . . .** If you have any unused marinade left over, it can be served with the salmon and salad. If it is too spicy, just add some more Greek yoghurt. Alternatively, you could serve the Feta Tzatziki (see page 109) as a very tasty accompaniment.

# MAPLE-GLAZED GAMMON WITH CHILLI PINEAPPLE SALSA AND CRUNCHY POTATOES

You have everything in this recipe to get your taste buds screaming for more: the natural saltiness from the gammon, the sweet maple syrup glaze, the juicy, tangy pineapple with a hint of spicy chilli and the sour kick from the rice vinegar. What more could you want? Well, a few crunchy potatoes on the side wouldn't go amiss.

• SERVES 2  • 1 HOUR

500g new potatoes

3 tablespoons olive oil

2 thick gammon steaks (see PS . . . )

sea salt and freshly ground black pepper

a small knob of butter

½ red chilli, deseeded and finely chopped

4 spring onions, chopped

½ small pineapple, cut into 5mm–1cm cubes

1 teaspoon rice vinegar

a handful of coriander, chopped

1 tablespoon maple syrup

Preheat the oven to 200°C/fan 180°C/gas 6.

Cook the potatoes in boiling salted water for 10 minutes. Drain and tip into a smallish roasting tray. Using a potato masher or the base of a glass/cup, crush each potato – some more than others so you get some lovely crispy bits once they have roasted. Toss in 2 tablespoons of olive oil and cook in the oven for about 45 minutes, turning a few times, until wonderfully golden and crunchy.

Once the potatoes have about 10 minutes to go, heat a frying pan with ½ tablespoon of olive oil. Season the gammon with pepper (salt shouldn't be necessary as the gammon will be salty enough) and cook for about 3 minutes each side. You might need less time if the steaks are particularly thin. If they are too big to fit in the pan, cut each one in half.

While you are frying the gammon, heat ½ tablespoon of olive oil and the butter in another frying pan. Add the chilli and spring onions, cooking for 1 minute before stirring in the pineapple and rice vinegar. Toss around for a minute or so for the pineapple to heat through and release some juices. Stir in the coriander and the salsa is ready.

To finish the gammon, pour in the maple syrup and let it bubble for a minute or so, turning the gammon a few times to get a sticky glaze.

Remove the potatoes from the oven and scatter with sea salt.

Serve the gammon with any maple glaze poured over and divide the salsa and potatoes between the two plates. Serve straight away.

**PS . . .** I like to use dry-cure or sweet-cure gammon. It shouldn't be too salty and has a lovely flavour.

# CINNAMON AND RAISIN RICE PUDDING WITH CARAMELIZED APPLES

I adore rice pudding and love the fact that it is so straightforward to make. Of course you can have just rice pudding, but the addition of cinnamon and raisins gives it a delicious, rich flavour and, when served with slices of caramelized apple, it is transformed into a very special midweek pudding.

• SERVES 2   • 20–25 MINUTES

*for the rice pudding*
75g risotto or pudding rice
200ml milk
150ml double cream
1 cinnamon stick,
  broken in half
½ teaspoon vanilla extract
50g raisins
1 tablespoon caster sugar

*for the apples*
10g butter
1 large eating apple, peeled,
  core removed and cut into
  thick slices
20g caster sugar

Place the rice, milk, cream, cinnamon, vanilla and raisins in a small non-stick saucepan. Bring to the boil over a medium heat and then turn down the heat until the creamy milk is just bubbling gently.

Leave to cook for 15 to 20 minutes, stirring frequently, until the rice has swelled and is soft, but still retains a little bite. Stir in the caster sugar and the rice pudding is ready.

While the pudding is cooking, over a medium to high heat, melt the butter in a frying pan and, once it is bubbling, fry the apple slices for a few minutes on both sides until golden. Increase the heat and sprinkle over the sugar and 1 tablespoon water. When the sauce begins to turn golden, stir the apples in the pan until they are coated in a sticky caramel.

Serve the rice pudding in bowls with the apples placed either on the top or to the side.

**PS . . .** A splash of Calvados (apple brandy) added to the apples with the sugar is a very tasty treat.

# BAKED PLUMS
# WITH PORT AND ORANGE MASCARPONE

Having a simple pudding recipe up your sleeve is essential and this won't disappoint anyone. Ripe greengages, apricots, peaches or nectarines can also be used.

• SERVES 2   • 30 MINUTES

6–10 (depending on their size) ripe plums

75g mascarpone cheese

grated zest of ½ orange

3 tablespoons port

2–3 tablespoons demerara sugar

a small handful of flaked almonds

Preheat the oven to 200°C/fan 180°C/gas 6.

Cut the plums in half and remove the stones. Sit, cut-side up, in a baking dish or roasting tray big enough so they are not overlapping, but not so large that they look lost.

Mix together the mascarpone cheese and grated orange. Place small spoons of the cheese on top of each plum and then pour over the port. Sprinkle the sugar and almonds over the top.

Place in the oven and bake for about 20 minutes until the plums are softened and golden on top. Serve hot or warm.

**PS . . .** The baked plums are delicious served with soft amaretti biscuits. You could also swap the port for a tawny port, sherry or even a Madeira.

# TIPSY ORANGES WITH VANILLA CREAM

For a really easy, light pudding option, this is a must. Not one for the drivers, though!

• SERVES 2   • 15 MINUTES, PLUS 30 MINUTES MARINATING

3–4 medium oranges
85ml sweet dessert wine
½ vanilla pod
125ml double cream
biscotti biscuits, to serve

Unless you have a super-sharp knife, you are best using a serrated bread knife to prepare the oranges – it makes the job really easy. Cut the top and bottom off the oranges and sit them on a board on one end. Slice away the peel and pith, working your way around each orange to reveal round, completely peeled oranges.

Slice each orange into thin rounds and place in a serving bowl with any juice from the board. Pour over the wine so the oranges are just covered and leave to marinate for a minimum of 30 minutes (but the longer you give them the better).

Split the half vanilla pod and scrape out the seeds into the cream. Stir to disperse the seeds and pour into a serving jug.

Serve the bowl of Tipsy Oranges at the table and offer the cream to pour over and a plate of the biscotti biscuits to dip into the delicious juice.

**PS . . .** Sliced peaches, nectarines or strawberries are a lovely alternative to the oranges. You can also use Grand Marnier, sloe gin or kirsch (with a little sugar added) instead of sweet wine. However, you'd be best to dilute this with some orange juice, otherwise you'll be on your back after tucking into a bowlful of oranges!

# MOCHA TOFFEE SUNDAES

This is a naughty treat to have midweek, but it is a good standby to turn to if you only have time to grab some basics on your way home.

• SERVES 2  • 10 MINUTES

2 Mars bars, chopped

2 tablespoons milk

2 tablespoons Tia Maria
  or brandy

50ml strong black coffee

vanilla ice-cream,
  as much as you fancy

4–6 HobNobs, digestives,
  chocolate cookies or your
  favourite biscuit, crumbled

Place the Mars bars in a small saucepan with the milk, Tia Maria or brandy and coffee and gently melt everything together to create a sauce. Once smooth, leave to cool slightly to thicken.

In two sundae glasses, glass dishes or one larger bowl to share, layer up the scoops of ice-cream, crumbled biscuits and mocha toffee sauce and serve straight away.

**PS . . .** If you are feeling a little guilty that you're not including any fruit in your dessert, then just add some sliced banana or even some tinned pears to the sundaes. But frankly, with all that ice-cream and chocolate, I wouldn't worry!

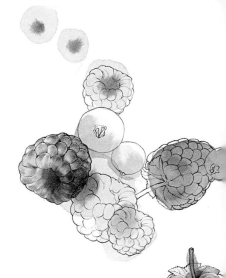

# RASPBERRY AND ELDERFLOWER SYLLABUB

What more can I say? Summer in a glass!

• SERVES 2   • 10 MINUTES, PLUS 30 MINUTES CHILLING

200g raspberries

1 tablespoon caster sugar

125ml double cream

1½ tablespoons
  elderflower cordial

75ml sweet dessert wine
  or sweet sherry

Place about 75g of the raspberries in a bowl with the caster sugar and crush with the back of a large spoon to release all of their lovely pink juices.

In a separate bowl, whip the cream until it is holding fairly firm peaks. Mix together the elderflower cordial and wine, then slowly whisk into the cream until you have a lovely thick yet light cream that will keep its shape. Fold in the crushed raspberries.

Spoon into some nice glasses (such as wine, martini or cocktail glasses) or pretty dishes with the fresh raspberries dotted among the spoons of syllabub.

Place in the fridge to chill for 30 minutes or more.

**PS . . .** Some light, crisp shortbread biscuits are a great accompaniment to enjoy with the syllabub.

# SPECIAL SATURDAY NIGHT DINNERS

*I've created two special menus for Saturday nights, so it's just like being in the kind of restaurant where you think, Do I have menu one or menu two? You might even find you need to flip a coin here. I would, however, recommend that you don't mix and match the menus, as the courses work brilliantly together.*

# Menu One

*Seared Tuna Carpaccio*
  *with Wasabi Dressing*

*Châteaubriand*
  *with Ginger and Chilli Marinade*

   *Baked Salt-spiced Chips*

   *Asian Coleslaw*

*Lime and Passion Fruit Cheesecakes*
  *with Coconut Crumbs*

\*And to drink . . .
  A soft fruity red, such as a New Zealand Pinot Noir, is just the ticket
  to match the mix of fish, meat and subtle spices in this menu.

# SEARED TUNA CARPACCIO WITH WASABI DRESSING

The flavours in this dish are so fresh and tasty and it's really straightforward to make. The tuna is just seared on the outside, leaving the inside lovely and tender. The simple salad is flavoured with a wasabi dressing, which adds a nice fiery bite.

• SERVES 2   • 15 MINUTES, PLUS 30 MINUTES CHILLING

100–125g piece of tuna loin, about 2–3cm thick

sea salt and freshly ground black pepper

1 tablespoon sesame seeds

3 tablespoons olive oil, plus an extra trickle for frying

8–10cm piece of cucumber

8 radishes

5–10 pieces of pickled ginger (depending on their size)

½ shallot, very thinly sliced

1 teaspoon lime juice

½ teaspoon wasabi paste

Season the tuna with salt and lots of freshly ground black pepper. Scatter the sesame seeds on a small plate, then roll the tuna in them to coat all over.

Heat a frying pan and, when it is nice and hot, add a trickle of oil and sear the tuna for 1½ minutes on all sides until it is nice and golden. Remove from the heat, transfer to a plate and place in the fridge to chill slightly for 30 minutes.

While the tuna is chilling, cut the cucumber in half lengthways and then very thinly slice into half-moon shapes. Place in a bowl. Slice the radishes as thinly as you can and add to the cucumber. If the ginger is in quite large slices, cut up a little smaller and toss with the radish and cucumber.

To make the dressing, mix together the shallot, lime juice, wasabi paste and remaining olive oil and season with a pinch of salt.

Remove the tuna from the fridge and slice thinly (about 5mm thick if you can). Lay the slices on two plates with the salad and then spoon over the dressing.

# CHÂTEAUBRIAND WITH GINGER AND CHILLI MARINADE

If you can get the steak from a butcher, ask for a nice rounded piece of meat from the centre of the fillet. It will cook evenly, melt in the mouth and look fabulous.

• SERVES 2  • 35 TO 40 MINUTES, PLUS 2 TO 4 HOURS MARINATING

½ long red chilli, deseeded

15–20g piece of fresh ginger, peeled

2 cloves of garlic

2 tablespoons olive oil

450–500g centre-cut beef fillet

sea salt

Preheat the oven to 200°C/fan 180°C/gas 6.

If you have a small food processor or blender, whizz together the chilli, ginger and garlic until they are finely chopped. If you don't, then just chop the ingredients as finely as you can . . . it won't take long, I promise!

Mix 1 tablespoon of the olive oil into the chilli, ginger and garlic, and then rub all over the steak. Wrap tightly in clingfilm, then leave in the fridge to marinate for about 2 to 4 hours.

When you are ready to cook the fillet, unwrap, rub off the marinade and season with salt.

Heat an ovenproof frying pan until it is almost smoking and then add the remaining 1 tablespoon of olive oil. Sear the fillet all over until it has a crusty, golden seal. This should only take about 2 to 3 minutes and is very easy if you hold the fillet with a pair of tongs to ensure even cooking.

Put the pan straight into the oven and cook for 20 minutes for medium-rare. Take out of the oven sooner for rare or leave for about 5 minutes more for medium–well done.

Remove from the oven and leave to rest for about 5 minutes or so before slicing and arranging on two plates. Serve with the Baked Salt-spiced Chips (see page 52) and the Asian Coleslaw (see page 53).

**PS . . .** The Châteaubriand can be cooked in the same way but without any marinade and served more traditionally with a béarnaise sauce (similar to a hollandaise, but flavoured with tarragon and vinegar rather than lemon juice). Serve with plain salted chips and watercress.

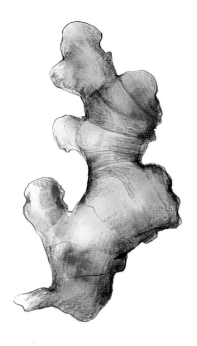

# BAKED SALT-SPICED CHIPS

You've got to have chips with your steak . . . it's the law.

• SERVES 2   • 45 MINUTES

450–550g peeled,
  medium-sized potatoes
¼ teaspoon hot
  chilli powder
½ teaspoon salt
2 tablespoons olive oil

Preheat the oven to 220°C/fan 200°C/gas 8.

Bring a pan of salted water to the boil.

Cut the potatoes into chips and place in the pan. Once the water returns to the boil, cook for 4 to 5 minutes. Drain, return the potatoes to the pan and then toss with the chilli powder, salt and oil. It doesn't matter if they start to crumble at the edges because this will give you some nice crunchy bits when they are cooked. Tip on to a baking tray and spread out in a single layer.

Place the chips in the oven to cook for about 30 to 35 minutes, turning a couple of times throughout, until crispy.

You shouldn't need any additional salt, so just serve straight away with the steak and Asian coleslaw.

**PS . . .** If you like vinegar on your chips, a nice alternative to fit in with the menu is to squeeze over a little lime juice instead.

# ASIAN COLESLAW

If you make this about 30 minutes before it's needed, the vegetables will have just started to soften and soak up the exceptionally tasty dressing.

• SERVES 2   • 10 MINUTES

½ small red onion
¼ red or white cabbage
1 carrot, peeled
2 tablespoons mayonnaise
1 tablespoon peanut butter
2 teaspoons rice vinegar
1 teaspoon fish sauce
1 tablespoon runny honey

With a sharp knife, slice the onion and cabbage as fine as you can. The carrot can be either cut into fine matchsticks or coarsely grated. Place these ingredients in a bowl.

In a separate bowl, mix together the mayonnaise, peanut butter, rice vinegar, fish sauce and honey. Mix into the vegetables and your coleslaw is ready to serve with the steak and chips.

# LIME AND PASSION FRUIT CHEESECAKES WITH COCONUT CRUMBS

Even though these are quite rich, the tanginess from the passion fruit and the lime makes them a lovely refreshing way to end your special Saturday dinner.

• SERVES 2   • 30 MINUTES, PLUS 30 MINUTES CHILLING

*for the coconut-crumb base*
15g desiccated coconut
20g butter
50g digestive biscuits

*for the cheesecake topping*
75g cream cheese
40g icing sugar
zest and juice of 1 lime
1 large ripe passion fruit
75ml double cream

*Two ramekin dishes
(approximately
150ml in capacity)*

To prepare the base, heat a small frying pan, add the coconut and gently toast until golden. Tip into a bowl and then add the butter to the pan to melt. Crush the biscuits to fine crumbs, either in a sealed sandwich bag with a rolling pin or in a small blender. Mix the crumbs and melted butter into the toasted coconut and divide between the two ramekin dishes. Press firmly with the base of a teaspoon and place in the fridge to cool.

To make the cheesecake topping, place the cream cheese in a mixing bowl and soften with a spatula or wooden spoon. Add the icing sugar, lime juice, three-quarters of the zest and three-quarters of the passion fruit pulp, keeping the remaining zest and passion fruit to garnish the finished cheesecakes. Mix well until the cheese is smooth.

In a separate bowl, whisk the cream until it forms soft peaks and then mix into the cream cheese mixture. Spoon into the ramekins and smooth the surface with a palette knife. Keep in the fridge for about 30 minutes or more to firm up.

When you are ready to serve, garnish the top of each cheesecake with the reserved lime zest and passion fruit pulp and enjoy!

# SPECIAL SATURDAY NIGHT DINNERS

*With asparagus, Parmesan, scallops, pancetta and chocolate, to name a few ingredients, this menu is perfect when you're feeling romantic – birthdays, Valentine's Day, anniversaries, or . . . just because.*

# Menu Two

*Asparagus*
  *with Crispy Parmesan and Anchovy Crumbs*

*Scallop and Pancetta Linguine*
  *with Lemon and Garlic Butter*

*Rich Chocolate Orange Mousse*

*\*And to drink . . .*
  A punchy, full-flavoured New World Sauvignon Blanc from Chile, South
  Africa or New Zealand will work a treat with both the asparagus and the
  lemony scallops.

# ASPARAGUS WITH CRISPY PARMESAN AND ANCHOVY CRUMBS

I suppose asparagus is a bit of an obvious ingredient to use if you want a romantic meal, but it really is delicious. I love to serve it simply coated in some salted butter, but cooked this way it is absolutely delectable and a little bit more substantial for a starter.

• SERVES 2   • 15 MINUTES

2 anchovies in olive oil, finely chopped

1 clove of garlic, crushed

2 tablespoons grated Parmesan cheese

25g white breadcrumbs

20g butter, melted

freshly ground black pepper

1 good-sized bunch of asparagus

Preheat the oven to 200°C/fan 180°C/gas 6.

Mix together the anchovies, garlic, Parmesan, breadcrumbs, butter and a twist of black pepper. Scatter into a small roasting tray or baking dish and cook in the oven for 5 minutes until the crumbs are just becoming golden and crispy.

Snap the asparagus about 2 to 4cm from the base of the stalks (they should naturally have a breaking point) and trim away any tough-looking pointy 'ears' on the stalks.

Cook the asparagus in boiling salted water for a few minutes until tender. Drain and pat dry with kitchen paper.

Remove the crumbs from the oven and spoon on to a plate. Place the asparagus in the roasting tray or dish and turn in any butter left there. Scatter the crumbs over the top and then place back in the oven for 8 to 10 minutes until the crumbs are a rich golden colour.

Serve straight away.

**PS . . .** If asparagus is out of season, you could fry or roast some portobello mushrooms until tender, then scatter with the partially baked crumbs and cook until they are golden and crunchy, as above.

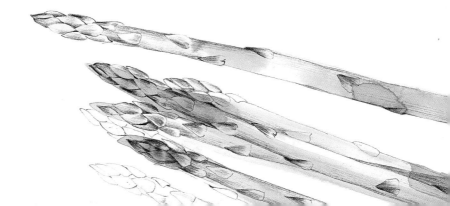

# SCALLOP AND PANCETTA LINGUINE WITH LEMON AND GARLIC BUTTER

This looks so sophisticated, yet is nice and easy to make. The number of scallops you serve is up to you, and of course it will depend on their size, but don't forget they are quite rich, especially when cooked with the lemon and garlic butter. This recipe would make a delicious starter to serve four, or even a pasta course if you are really going to town for a dinner party.

• SERVES 2   • 20 MINUTES

200g linguine

75g butter,
  at room temperature

2 cloves of garlic, crushed

grated zest and juice
  of ½ lemon

2 tablespoons finely
  chopped parsley

150g diced pancetta

6–12 scallops, with or
  without the roe attached
  (it's up to you)

sea salt and freshly ground
  black pepper

Cook the linguine until al dente.

Meanwhile, mix together the butter, garlic, lemon zest and parsley and keep to one side.

In a small to medium frying pan, fry the pancetta over a low heat until the fat becomes crispy. Remove with a slotted spoon and drain on kitchen paper. Pour away any excess fat in the pan and then increase the heat.

Season the scallops with salt and pepper and cook in the frying pan for 1 minute each side, turning them in the order they were put into the pan. They should be lightly golden and slightly springy to the touch. Add half of the flavoured butter and cook with the scallops for about 30 seconds to coat them.

Drain the pasta and toss in the remaining butter and the pancetta. Divide the linguine between two plates, top with the scallops and finish off with a squeeze of the lemon juice.

**PS . . .** Frozen scallops can be used for this recipe, so don't panic if you can't get any fresh ones.

# RICH CHOCOLATE ORANGE MOUSSE

You won't want anything too heavy to finish off this meal and I think this deliciously simple chocolate mousse is perfect. There isn't any cream added to the mousse, which makes it wonderfully chocolatey yet exceptionally rich − therefore the relatively small portions are essential (chocoholics may disagree!).

• SERVES 2   • 10 MINUTES, PLUS 30 MINUTES CHILLING

75g dark chocolate
   (about 70% cocoa solids)

1 egg, separated

20g caster sugar

1 tablespoon orange liqueur,
   such as Grand Marnier
   or Cointreau

grated or shaved chocolate
   to garnish

Break the chocolate into small pieces and melt in a small bowl over a pan of just-simmering water, making sure the bowl isn't touching the water. As soon as it has melted, remove the bowl from the heat and leave the chocolate to cool for a few minutes.

Meanwhile, whisk the egg white until it reaches soft peaks and then add the sugar. Continue to whisk until the whites are thick and glossy.

Stir the egg yolk and orange liqueur into the chocolate and then mix in a third of the egg whites to loosen the mixture. Very gently fold in the remainder of the whites until you have a thick and rich chocolate mousse.

Spoon into small coffee cups, wine glasses or even small ramekin dishes or glass bowls (they need to have about 75ml capacity) and place into the fridge to chill for about 30 minutes or so.

When you are ready to serve the mousses, sit them on a saucer or plate and garnish with some grated or shaved chocolate.

**PS . . .** Feel free to add a splash of your favourite tipple, such as brandy, whisky, Malibu, rum, Tia Maria, Amaretto, etc., instead of the orange liqueur.

# TEA FOR TWO

*All together now – 'Tea for two and two for tea . . .'*
*They made a film about this, so clearly it's a very*
*important form of entertaining. Get yourself a cake*
*stand, choose some nice leaf tea, perhaps employ*
*a pianist and get your best friend round. Sticking*
*your pinky out is mandatory.*

# Menu

*St Clement's Drizzle Cake*

*Maple and Cinnamon Kisses*

*Double Chocolate Freezer Cookies*

*Baked Portuguese Custard Tarts*

*Strawberries and Cream Swiss Roll*

*Pistachio and Raspberry Macaroons*

# ST CLEMENT'S DRIZZLE CAKE

My grandma made the best lemon drizzle cake ever, so here it is with my little twist (the addition of orange). You'll love it.

• SERVES 2   • 15 MINUTES, PLUS 30–45 MINUTES BAKING

175g caster sugar

175g softened butter

grated zest and juice of 1 large lemon

grated zest and juice of 1 large orange

4 tablespoons milk

2 eggs

175g self-raising flour

3 tablespoons granulated sugar

Preheat the oven to 180°C/fan 160°C/gas 4.

Grease and line the base of 1 large (900g) or 2 small (450g) loaf tins.

Place the caster sugar, butter and the zest of the lemon and orange in a bowl and beat together until pale and creamy. Add the milk, and then beat in the eggs, one at a time, with a spoon of flour to prevent the mixture from curdling. Mix in the remaining flour. Spoon into the prepared tin/tins and level the surface flat.

Bake in the oven for about 45 minutes for a large cake or 30 minutes for the smaller cakes until they are golden and a skewer comes out clean when inserted into the centre of the cake. Don't worry if you see the cake peak in the middle and split – it all adds character and will also give you a crunchier drizzle topping.

While the cake is cooking, place the lemon and orange juice in a saucepan, bring to the boil and allow to reduce in quantity to about 3 tablespoons. Leave to cool, and then stir in the granulated sugar so it just starts to dissolve.

As soon as the cake comes out of the oven, prick several times with a skewer, then slowly pour the lemon and orange sugar all over the top, letting it soak into the cake. Leave to cool completely in the tin before turning out and cutting into slices to serve.

**PS . . .** The cake will stay fresh for 3 to 4 days in an airtight container, but will also freeze really well, so it is perfect to have as a Tea for Two standby saviour.

# MAPLE AND CINNAMON KISSES

I used to love making chocolate kisses with my sister, Millie, when we were little, so we reminisced one afternoon and came up with these little beauties. I hope you enjoy them as much as we both do.

• MAKES 20  • 30 MINUTES

*for the biscuits*

150g self-raising flour

½ teaspoon ground cinnamon

75g caster sugar

75g butter

1 egg, beaten

1 tablespoon maple syrup

*for the buttercream*

50g icing sugar, plus extra for dusting

75g butter, at room temperature

4 tablespoons maple syrup

*You will also need a piping bag and large star-shaped nozzle*

Preheat the oven to 180°C/fan 160°C/gas 4.

For speed and ease, place the flour, cinnamon, sugar and butter in a food processor and blitz to combine. Add the egg and maple syrup and briefly blitz so everything comes together to a paste. This can also be done by hand, rubbing the butter into the dry ingredients before adding the egg and maple syrup. It's not exactly difficult, but a little messier and takes slightly longer.

Using a piping bag and large star-shaped nozzle, pipe twenty rosettes on to one or two baking trays lined with non-stick parchment paper. You don't need to leave a large gap between each biscuit because they won't spread too much. Place in the oven for about 15 minutes until lightly golden. Once cooked, remove from the trays and cool on a wire rack.

To make the buttercream filling, sift the icing sugar into a bowl and beat together with the butter and maple syrup until pale and creamy. Put into the piping bag with the same star nozzle (both of which need to be washed and dried first). Pipe a decent-sized blob of the buttercream on to the base of half the biscuits and sandwich together with the remaining biscuits. Dust with icing sugar and store in an airtight container if you don't plan on eating them straight away.

**PS . . .** To make Coffee Kisses, replace the cinnamon with 2 teaspoons instant coffee dissolved in 1 tablespoon hot water and add with the egg.

# DOUBLE CHOCOLATE FREEZER COOKIES

Freshly baked cookies, still warm from the oven, are virtually impossible to resist, so what could be better than having some cookie dough in the freezer to create instant home-made cookies to enjoy with a cuppa? These are light and crispy on the edges, but still remain slightly soft and chewy in the middle. In my book, that is what's otherwise known as 'perfect'.

• MAKES 12   • 20 MINUTES, PLUS 15 MINUTES BAKING

125g softened butter

100g caster sugar

1 teaspoon vanilla extract

1 egg yolk

125g plain flour,
   plus extra for dusting

15g cocoa powder

75g milk chocolate,
   chopped or broken
   into smallish chunks

1 tablespoon grated plain
   or milk chocolate

Place the butter and sugar in an electric mixer or food processor and blend together until pale and creamy. Add the vanilla extract and egg yolk and whizz together briefly before sifting in the flour and cocoa powder. Mix until you have a smooth dough and finally add the chunks of chocolate.

Using lightly floured hands, roughly roll the dough into golf-sized balls and gently press each one in the palm of your hand. Place on a small, clingfilm-lined baking tray or something similar that will sit flat in your freezer. Leave in your freezer for about 1 hour for the dough to become solid, then peel away from the clingfilm. Place the uncooked cookies in a freezer bag or container to store for up to 2 months.

When you want to bake some of the cookies, preheat the oven to 200°C/fan 180°C/gas 6.

Remove as many as you wish from the freezer and place on a greased baking tray, making sure they are spread slightly apart.

Bake for about 15 minutes until they are just beginning to firm up, but haven't become too dark around the edges (there's nothing worse than a slightly burnt, bitter-tasting chocolate cookie). Remove from the oven, sprinkle the tops with the grated chocolate and let cool for a couple of minutes before cooling further on a wire rack.

**PS . . .** The cookies can be cooked as soon as they are made. They will take just 10 to 12 minutes in the oven. These quantities will easily double up to make plenty for your freezer . . . ideal for those unexpected sweet-craving moments.

# BAKED PORTUGUESE CUSTARD TARTS

The best thing about these is that the custard is deliciously rich, but the filo pastry is lovely and light. The perfect excuse to have more than one, I reckon!

• MAKES 9  • 30 MINUTES, PLUS 25 MINUTES BAKING

*for the filling*

3 egg yolks
125g caster sugar
2 tablespoons cornflour
225ml double cream
175ml milk
1 teaspoon vanilla extract

*for the pastry*

50g butter
1 tablespoon caster sugar
¼ teaspoon freshly
   grated nutmeg
¼ teaspoon ground
   cinnamon
8 sheets, or approximately
   120g, filo pastry

Preheat the oven to 180°C/fan 160°C/gas 4.

Place the egg yolks, caster sugar and cornflour in a non-stick saucepan and mix together. Add the cream, milk and vanilla extract, whisking until smooth with a balloon whisk.

Place over a medium heat and cook, stirring, until the custard thickens and just comes to the boil. Remove from the heat and cover the surface of the custard with clingfilm to prevent a skin forming.

For the pastry, melt the butter and then stir in the sugar, nutmeg and cinnamon.

Lay a piece of filo pastry on the worktop and brush with the butter. Lay another piece on top, brush with butter and continue to do the same with a third and fourth sheet of pastry. Using a sharp knife, cut out as many 10cm squares of this pastry as you can. Continue to do the same with the remaining sheets of filo, brushing with the butter, so you basically end up with about nine 10cm squares, each with four layers of the filo.

Press each square into the holes of a deep muffin tin. Spoon the cooled custard into the pastry cases and bake for 25 minutes until the pastry is golden and crisp and the custard is beginning to become golden.

Leave in the tin for a few minutes before transferring to a wire rack to cool.

**PS . . .** If you're not planning on eating all of these on the day they are cooked, they will keep fresh for a day or two, but avoid putting them in an airtight container because the pastry will go soft. Keep loosely covered in a cool place (not the fridge).

# STRAWBERRIES AND CREAM SWISS ROLL

This is my take on the classic Victoria sandwich – vanilla sponge, cream and strawberries. As well as serving this with tea, you could also serve it as a dessert.

• MAKES 1 SWISS ROLL, GIVING 4 LARGE SLICES   • 40 MINUTES

4 eggs
100g caster sugar
100g self-raising flour
caster sugar, for dusting

*for the filling*
150ml double cream
25g caster sugar
seeds from 1 vanilla pod
100g strawberries,
   thinly sliced, plus
   a few extra to garnish

*You will also need a Swiss
roll tin measuring about
25cm x 15cm*

Line the Swiss roll tin with non-stick parchment paper, leaving the edges sticking up over the sides to allow for the rising of the sponge when cooking.

Preheat the oven to 180°C/fan 160°C/gas 4.

Using an electric mixer, whisk together the eggs and sugar for about 5 minutes until the mixture is pale and creamy, doubling in volume. Sift the flour and carefully fold in a little at a time to prevent any lumps forming in the mixture. Pour into the prepared tin, spreading it evenly into the corners. Bake in the oven for 10 to 12 minutes until the sponge is just golden and lightly springy to the touch.

Cut a piece of parchment paper slightly bigger than the sponge and dust heavily with caster sugar. Turn the sponge upside down on to the sugared surface and carefully peel away the lining parchment. Leave to cool, covered with a tea towel.

To make the filling, whisk together the cream, sugar and seeds from the vanilla pod until the cream forms fairly firm peaks. Spread over the sponge, leaving about a 2cm border to allow for spreading when rolling. Lay the sliced strawberries on top, then gently roll the sponge along its length to form a thick log. Make sure the seam of the sponge is facing down and transfer to a serving plate.

Garnish with extra strawberries and serve in thick slices.

**PS . . .** You don't have to fill the cake with fresh cream and strawberries. Good-quality strawberry, raspberry or even cherry jam is really delicious with some vanilla buttercream. Serve with a dollop of crème fraîche.

# PISTACHIO AND RASPBERRY MACAROONS

Twelve macaroons for two? You're going to have to be strong here. Perhaps share them with your neighbours or take some to work to give to your boss.

• **MAKES 12 MEDIUM-SIZED MACAROONS** • **45 MINUTES**

100g shelled unsalted
  pistachios

175g icing sugar

2 egg whites

green food colouring (optional)

about 4 tablespoons
  good-quality raspberry jam

2 tablespoons clotted cream

*You will also need a piping
  bag with a 1cm nozzle
  and a couple of baking
  trays lined with non-stick
  parchment paper and
  lightly brushed with oil*

Preheat the oven to 170°C/fan 150°C/gas 3.

Place all but about 15g of the pistachios in a food processor, sift in half of the icing sugar and blitz to fine crumbs. The rest of the pistachios can be chopped fairly finely and kept to one side.

In a large mixing bowl, whisk the egg whites until they form stiff peaks. Sieve in the remaining icing sugar and continue to whisk until the meringue becomes glossy. A minute should be fine.

Using a large metal spoon, fold the ground pistachios into the meringue with a few drops of green food colouring if you are using it.

Spoon into the piping bag and pipe twenty-four round blobs (about 4cm in diameter) on to the lined baking tray, leaving a small space between each. Add a little sprinkling of pistachios on top of half of the meringues. Now leave to stand for about 10 minutes to allow a 'skin' to form on top and prevent them from spreading too much in the oven.

Place in the oven and cook for 15 minutes, or until they are firm but not coloured. Remove from the oven and leave to cool.

When cold, sandwich the macaroons in pairs with a little raspberry jam on one side and clotted cream on the other, making sure each pair has a pistachio-sprinkled top.

Serve in little cake cases or on a plate. They will keep for a day or two once made.

# CHAPTER TWO
# RELAXED ENTERTAINING

For those of you who love informal entertaining, your usual menu is about to be updated. For my Girls' Night In, I've sorted the recipes and you're going to love them. Think sparkly, indulgent, spicy and colourful. So, send your invites out, order the wine, buy a new outfit and get rid of any males until at least the following morning.

Now, for my Boys' Night In, I've had to have help from the males I know, so if I've got it wrong, my husband and his mates are for it. Apparently card nights are the 'in thing'. (Although I don't think my male friends have ever been to one. They just like the idea.) I've got all the usual boy things covered – steak, flavoured butters, mash, whisky, onion rings, etc. I've even looked into the rules of Texas Hold 'em – in fact, I think I might hold a boys' night in for my girlfriends.

Friday (for me) is the best night of the week for relaxed entertaining because I've usually got the weekend off. I get the wine out, whip up something lovely and chill out with my husband and a couple of friends. (You can stay up late on Fridays, it's allowed.)

It's believed that the tradition of Sunday lunch arose because the meat could be left in the oven before church and was therefore ready when the family arrived home at lunch-time. Whatever you do on a Sunday – go to church, go for a long walk, wash the car or go down to the pub – you'll hopefully like my versions of the most sociable and traditional lunch of the week.

That's the second chapter. Oh . . . if any boys out there have a card night, do let me know. I really have looked at the rules of Texas Hold 'em.

# GIRLS' NIGHT IN

*This is all about grazing food – things to pick at and nibble on throughout the evening. You'll love the drinks and the Tomato Tatins, the popcorn goes brilliantly with any film, and Chicken Kiev Nuggets are a delicious blast from the past. It's going to be a good night. Not sure if I need to add anything else, other than: behave irresponsibly and perhaps organize it for a weekend.*

# Menu

*Mini Tomato Tatins*

*＊Watermelon Martinis*

*Parmesan and Pecan Crisps*

*Spiced Chips 'n' Dips*

*Cheesy Chilli Popcorn*

*＊Apple Sparkle Cocktail*

*Crab and Crayfish Cocktails*

*Chicken Kiev Nuggets*

*Limoncello Jellies
  with Mint Cream*

*Cappuccino Knickerbocker Glories*

*Very Indulgent Cupcakes*

# MINI TOMATO TATINS

If you want to make these ahead of time, prepare the caramelized tomatoes, divide between the patty tins and, once cool, top with the pastry. Keep in the fridge until you are ready to cook them, then just give them a couple more minutes in the oven than stated below.

• MAKES 24  • 20 MINUTES

25g butter

2 large shallots, thinly sliced

2 tablespoons caster sugar

2 tablespoons balsamic vinegar

24 cherry tomatoes, halved

sea salt and freshly ground black pepper

375g ready-rolled puff pastry

1–2 sprigs of thyme

*You will also need one or two twelve-hole non-stick patty tins or bun trays and one or two flat, heavy baking trays*

Preheat the oven to 200°C/fan 180°C/gas 6.

Melt the butter in a smallish frying pan. Sauté the shallots over a gentle heat until they are softened. Increase the heat and stir in the sugar and balsamic vinegar and cook for about 30 seconds to a minute until the shallots are slightly caramelized and sticky.

Add the cherry tomatoes and cook for 1 to 2 minutes until they are just beginning to soften. Remove from the heat and season with salt and pepper.

Cut out twenty-four circles of pastry about 5cm in diameter either with a pastry cutter or by cutting around a glass with a sharp knife.

Divide the tomatoes and shallots among the holes in the patty tins. Scatter a few thyme leaves into each one and then lay a circle of puff pastry on top, pressing it into the hole lightly. If you have just one tin, then you will need to bake these in two batches. Grease the baking trays with a little oil and sit them directly on top of the bun trays. This might seem a little strange, but it will make the pastry nice and crisp and also stopping it from rising.

Place in the oven and cook for 12 minutes. Once cooked, turn both the patty tins and the baking trays upside-down so the trays are on the bottom. Leave for a minute or so and then carefully lift off the patty tins. You may need to coax the pastry off some of the tatins, but what you should have is twenty-four super-flat pastry bases, each topped with juicy, caramelized tomatoes.

Serve warm.

# WATERMELON MARTINIS

This is a delicious, refreshing twist on the classic Cosmopolitan.

• MAKES 6   • 15 MINUTES

500g watermelon flesh
150ml vodka
60ml Chambord
 (raspberry liqueur)
60ml fresh lime juice
ice
thin slices/wedges of
 watermelon, to garnish

Blend the watermelon to a smooth juice and strain through a sieve. You should have about 300ml juice. This can be made well ahead of time and kept in the fridge.

Using a cocktail shaker, make two martinis at a time. Place 100ml watermelon juice, 50ml vodka, 20ml Chambord, 20ml lime juice and a good handful of ice in the shaker. Shake well and strain into two martini glasses. Garnish each glass with a piece of watermelon.

Continue making the rest of the martinis. Cheers.

PS . . . If you can't find Chambord, other fruit liqueurs will work nicely, such as crème de cassis, crème de mure or a strawberry liqueur.

# PARMESAN AND PECAN CRISPS

Delicate and tasty – just like us girls.

• MAKES 20 TO 24 CRISPS   • 10 MINUTES

80g Parmesan cheese,
 finely grated
40g pecan nuts,
 very finely chopped
a good pinch of cayenne
 pepper

Preheat the oven to 200°C/fan 180°C/gas 6.

Mix all of the ingredients together.

Line a couple of baking trays with non-stick parchment paper. Place teaspoonfuls of the Parmesan and pecan mixture on the baking trays, leaving a 3 to 4cm gap between each to allow for spreading.

Cook in the oven for 5 to 7 minutes until the crisps are evenly golden and bubbling. Remove and leave to cool on the baking tray. Peel off the parchment paper and store flat in an airtight container until you are ready to serve them.

PS . . . If you like things spicy, check out the Jalepeño and Parmesan Crisps from the Boys' Night In section on page 99.

# SPICED CHIPS 'N' DIPS

It's not a girls' night in without the all-time favourite – chips. Serve them coated in different spices with accompanying dips and they're guaranteed to be a real hit.

• SERVES 6 TO 8    • 10 MINUTES, PLUS 40–45 MINUTES IN THE OVEN

6–8 large potatoes, cut into chip shapes or long, slim wedges

3 tablespoons sunflower oil

1 tablespoon sesame oil

2 tablespoons Thai seven-spice seasoning (Chinese five-spice can be used as an alternative)

sea salt

¼ teaspoon ground turmeric

2 teaspoons garam masala

½ teaspoon chilli powder

sweet chilli dipping sauce, to serve

bought raita or mango chutney, to serve

Preheat the oven to 200°C/fan 180°C/gas 6.

To make the Thai-spiced chips, toss half of the potato chips or wedges in 1 tablespoon of the sunflower oil, the sesame oil, Thai seven-spice seasoning and a pinch of salt. Place on a non-stick baking tray.

For the Indian-spiced chips, toss the remaining potato chips or wedges with the rest of the sunflower oil, the turmeric, garam masala, chilli powder and a good pinch of salt. Place on a separate non-stick baking tray.

Place both trays in the oven and bake for about 40 to 45 minutes until crispy, turning a couple of times part-way through.

Serve with a bowl of sweet chilli dipping sauce to dip the Thai chips into and some raita or mango chutney to dip the Indian-spiced chips into.

# CHEESY CHILLI POPCORN

Be warned, this is very moreish.

• SERVES 4 TO 6   • 10 MINUTES

50g Parmesan cheese,
   finely grated
1 teaspoon chilli powder
½ teaspoon salt
vegetable or sunflower oil
75g popping corn

Mix together the Parmesan, chilli powder and salt and keep to one side.

Place a large saucepan over a high heat. Once it is hot, add enough oil to just cover the bottom of the pan (about 3 tablespoons should be plenty). Stir in the popcorn until it is coated in the oil. Cover the pan with a lid and wait a minute or two for the popping (and fun) to start. Shake the pan a couple of times while the corn pops and, as soon as the popping stops, remove the pan from the heat.

Sprinkle over the chilli Parmesan. Stir or toss thoroughly until the cheese lightly coats the popcorn and serve either warm or cool.

**PS . . .** This makes a great gift to take round to a friend's house for a night in and a perfect lower-fat alternative to crisps.

# APPLE SPARKLE COCKTAIL

Because sparkly things are essential on a girls' night in.

• MAKES 6   • 5 MINUTES

200ml gin
100ml elderflower cordial
300ml sparkling apple juice
400ml soda water
ice
sprigs of mint, to garnish

Mix together the gin, elderflower cordial, apple juice and soda water.

Fill six tall glasses with ice and pour in the cocktail. Garnish with mint and serve.

# CRAB AND CRAYFISH COCKTAILS

The girls will love this contemporary version of the classic prawn cocktail, especially when served in supercool glasses.

• SERVES 6 TO 8   • 5 MINUTES

2 Baby Gem lettuces,
   finely shredded

4 spring onions,
   very thinly sliced

sea salt and freshly
   ground black pepper

½ lemon

100–150g fresh or tinned
   white crabmeat

about 150g crayfish tails
   (available in brine from
   many supermarkets,
   or prawns can be used
   as an alternative)

cayenne pepper

6–8 tablespoons bought
   seafood sauce

caviar, to garnish
   (see PS . . . )

In a bowl, mix together the Baby Gems and spring onions, then season with salt and pepper and a squeeze of lemon juice.

Season the crabmeat and crayfish with salt, a pinch of cayenne pepper and a squeeze of lemon juice.

Layer the Baby Gems, crabmeat, crayfish and seafood sauce in six to eight dishes or glasses and finish with a sprinkle of cayenne pepper and a small spoonful of caviar on top.

Keep chilled until needed and, when ready, serve with small forks or spoons.

**PS . . .** Onuga caviar and salmon caviar are wonderful ingredients to use as a garnish. They're relatively inexpensive and look very indulgent.

# CHICKEN KIEV NUGGETS

It's a girly night in, with no boys, so who cares about the garlic?

• 18 NUGGETS  • 30 MINUTES

2 skinless, boneless
  chicken breasts
4 cloves of garlic
a small bunch of parsley
a small bunch of chives
grated zest of ½ lemon
3 eggs
sea salt and freshly ground
  black pepper
4 tablespoons plain flour
200g dried
  natural breadcrumbs
5 tablespoons olive oil
50g butter
lemon wedges, to serve
mayonnaise, to serve
  (optional)

Roughly chop the chicken, garlic and herbs and place in a food processor with the lemon zest and white of just one egg (keep the yolk for later). Add a good pinch of salt and some pepper and blitz until you have a coarse paste.

Using slightly damp hands, shape the mixture into about eighteen nuggets.

Mix the reserved egg yolk with the two whole eggs in a shallow bowl. Place the flour and breadcrumbs, separately, in two more shallow bowls.

Lightly coat the nuggets with flour, then dip each one into the beaten egg and coat with the crumbs. Repeat the egg and crumb process so they all have a double coating. The nuggets can be placed in the fridge at this stage and cooked when needed.

Heat the oil in a large frying pan and, once it is hot, fry the nuggets for about 8 minutes, turning halfway through, until they are golden. Add the butter to the pan and turn the nuggets so they have a coating of the bubbling butter.

Serve straight away with a wedge of lemon to squeeze over and some mayonnaise for dipping if you fancy.

# LIMONCELLO JELLIES WITH MINT CREAM

These delicious, light desserts are ideal for cutting down on last-minute panics since they need to be made well ahead of time. They are quite potent, so don't offer them to any drivers.

• SERVES 6 TO 8 • 10 MINUTES, PLUS 4 HOURS OR OVERNIGHT SETTING IN THE FRIDGE

*for the jellies*

6 leaves of gelatine

200ml freshly squeezed lemon juice (from about 6 lemons)

100g caster sugar

300ml limoncello

*for the cream*

125ml double cream

25g caster sugar

2 tablespoons finely chopped mint

6–8 sprigs of mint, to garnish

Place the gelatine leaves in 200ml cold water to soften for a few minutes.

Strain the lemon juice into a saucepan and place over a gentle heat. Add the sugar and stir until it has dissolved.

Remove the gelatine leaves from the water and stir them into the hot lemon juice until they have completely dissolved. Add the water they were soaking in and finally stir in the limoncello.

Divide among six to eight nice wine or cocktail glasses and place in the fridge for at least 4 hours, but ideally overnight, to set.

Before serving, whip the cream until it is starting to thicken. Add the sugar and chopped mint and continue to whip until it reaches a soft dolloping consistency.

Remove the jellies from the fridge and spoon a little of the cream on top of each one. Add a sprig of mint and serve.

**PS . . .** If you are serving these as your only sweet treat, it is nice to offer some crisp shortbread biscuits on the side.

# CAPPUCCINO KNICKERBOCKER GLORIES

There's no precise recipe to follow here – it is entirely up to you how much you put into each tall glass. Enjoy being extravagant, layering up the vanilla and coffee ice-cream, espresso syrup, banana, meringue, whipped cream and chocolate-crusted pecans.

• MAKES UP TO 8   • 25 MINUTES

100g pecan nuts,
    broken into pieces
2 tablespoons caster sugar
1 tablespoon cocoa powder
vanilla ice-cream
coffee ice-cream
sliced banana
ready-made meringues,
    broken into bits
1 quantity of espresso syrup
    (see Ricotta and Coconut
    Hotcakes with Espresso
    Syrup, page 16)
whipped cream
over-the-top suggestions
    to serve include sparklers,
    cherries, wafers, etc.

The crunchy chocolate pecans can be prepared days in advance and stored in an airtight container. Heat a medium frying pan over a low to medium heat, add the nuts and toss around to toast lightly for a minute or two. Mix together the sugar and cocoa and sift over the top. Continue to toss around until the sugar melts and coats the nuts. Tip on to a plate lined with greaseproof paper and leave to cool. Break up any nuts that have stuck together.

When you are ready to indulge in the knickerbocker glories, layer up the ice-creams, banana and meringue, drizzling the espresso syrup in between the layers.

Top with a spoon of whipped cream and scatter over the nuts. Serve as they are or garnish to your heart's content!

**PS . . .** A splash of coffee liqueur or Baileys goes down rather well among the layers.

# VERY INDULGENT CUPCAKES

These are the ultimate girls' night in treat, but, it has to be said, they are equally delicious to enjoy over morning coffee, afternoon tea, at a celebration or even as an alternative to dessert. In fact, it's hard to think of a time when they aren't suitable.

• MAKES 12   • 1 HOUR 20 MINUTES

*for vanilla cupcakes*

175g caster sugar

175g unsalted butter,
   at room temperature

1 teaspoon vanilla extract

3 eggs

175g self-raising flour

*for vanilla icing*

200g unsalted butter,
   at room temperature

400g icing sugar, sifted

1 teaspoon vanilla extract

*You will also need a deep
   muffin tin and twelve paper
   muffin cases, and a piping
   bag with a wide star nozzle*

Preheat the oven to 180ºC/fan 160ºC/gas 4.

To make the cupcakes, beat together the sugar, butter and vanilla extract using an electric mixer until the mixture is wonderfully light and fluffy. Give this plenty of time because the creamier the mixture, the lighter the cakes. Add one egg at a time with a spoonful of flour to stop the mixture from curdling. Finally, mix in the remaining flour.

Spoon the cake mixture into twelve muffin cases sitting in the muffin tin. Cook in the oven for 20 minutes, until the cakes have risen and are lightly golden.

Remove from the oven and cool on a wire rack.

While the cakes are cooling, beat together the butter, icing sugar and vanilla extract until it is light and creamy. Place in a piping bag with a wide star nozzle and pipe a wonderfully generous swirl on top of each cupcake.

**PS . . .** If you are making the cake mixture in a food processor, then it is worth adding 1 teaspoon baking powder to the mixture to ensure the cakes rise nicely.

## Customize Your Cakes

Here are a few ideas for some other flavours for the sponge:

*Chocolate* Substitute 40g flour for 40g sieved cocoa powder.

*Lemon* Beat the grated rind of 1 lemon in with the sugar and butter and swap the milk for lemon juice.

*Orange* Beat the grated rind of 1 orange in with the sugar and butter and swap the milk for orange juice.

*Spice* Stir 2 teaspoons mixed spice into the flour.

And a few ideas for flavouring the icing:

*Dark chocolate* (best cupcake match – chocolate, orange or vanilla).
Add 100g melted dark chocolate.

*White chocolate* (best cupcake match – chocolate, vanilla, orange or spice).
Add 100g melted white chocolate.

*Orange flower* (best cupcake match – spice, vanilla or lemon).
Add ½ teaspoon orange flower water and a few drops of orange food colouring (or red and yellow combined).

*Lemon* (best cupcake match – orange, lemon or vanilla).
Add the juice and grated zest of 1 small lemon, plus a few drops of yellow food colouring.

*Rose* (best cupcake match – vanilla, lemon or orange).
Add ½ teaspoon rose water and a few drops of pink food colouring.

*Mint* (best cupcake match – chocolate or orange).
Add 1 teaspoon natural peppermint extract and a few drops of green food colouring.

*Coffee* (best cupcake match – chocolate, vanilla or spice).
Add 1 tablespoon coffee granules dissolved in 1 tablespoon hot water.

*Cinnamon* (best cupcake match – orange, vanilla, chocolate or spice).
Add 1 to 2 teaspoons ground cinnamon, depending on how strong you would like the flavour to be.

# BOYS' NIGHT IN

*I think the only ingredients missing from your boys'*
*night in are some 'Allowed Out' passes from your*
*wives and girlfriends, and a croupier.*

# Menu

*Hot and Spicy Nuts*

*Jalapeño and Parmesan Crisps*

*Pork, Stilton and Port Pies*
    *Root Vegetable and Mustard Mash*

*Toasted Ciabatta with Roasted Garlic*

*Steak Night*
    *Beer-battered Onion Rings*

*Half-pounder Greek Lamb Burgers*

*Tomato Spiced Mussels and Spaghetti*

*Whisky Bread-and-butter Pudding*

# HOT AND SPICY NUTS

A fantastic recipe to kick off your boys' night in. Make sure there's plenty of beer on hand as they can be quite spicy, and please act responsibly when adding the chilli powder!

• SERVES 8  • 15 MINUTES

1 egg white

400g mixed nuts,
    such as brazils, almonds,
    pecans and cashews

1 teaspoon hot chilli powder

½ teaspoon salt

2 tablespoons
    demerara sugar

Preheat the oven to 200°C/fan 180°C/gas 6.

In a large bowl, lightly whisk the egg white until it is frothy. Add the nuts, chilli powder, salt and sugar. Stir until the nuts are evenly coated.

Spread the nuts out on a lightly oiled non-stick baking tray, making sure they're in a single layer. Cook in the oven for 8 to 10 minutes until the mixture has dried.

Allow to cool and break up any nuts that have stuck together.

# JALAPEÑO AND PARMESAN CRISPS

Crisps . . . jalapeños . . . Parmesan . . . together? 'Oh my God!' I hear you shout. Yes, this is a little slice (in the form of a crisp) of heaven in one bite.

• **MAKES 20 TO 24 CRISPS** • **10 MINUTES**

15–20g jalapeño peppers
    from a jar
80g Parmesan cheese,
    finely grated

Preheat the oven to 200°C/fan 180°C/gas 6.

Dry the jalapeño peppers on kitchen paper, finely chop and mix with the Parmesan.

Line a couple of baking trays with non-stick parchment paper. Place teaspoonfuls of the Parmesan and jalapeño mixture on the baking trays, leaving a 3 to 4cm gap between each to allow for spreading.

Cook in the oven for 5 to 7 minutes, until the crisps are evenly golden and bubbling. Remove and leave to cool on the baking tray. Peel off the parchment paper and store flat in an airtight container until you are ready to serve them.

**PS . . .** If you like the sound of these, why not give the girls' version a go, too (see page 82)?

# PORK, STILTON AND PORT PIES

I know you boys like your pies. These are full of flavour and make a really hearty meal when served with the Root Vegetable and Mustard Mash (see page 102). They can easily be made ahead and kept in the fridge, so no last-minute chaos in the kitchen.

• SERVES 4   • 1 HOUR, PLUS UP TO 2 HOURS MARINATING

500g pork fillet
2–3 sprigs of thyme
150ml white port
    (dry sherry could
    be used as an alternative)
2 cloves of garlic, crushed
40g dried cranberries
sea salt and freshly
    ground black pepper
2 tablespoons olive oil
1 onion, thinly sliced
100g chestnut mushrooms,
    sliced
100ml double cream
200ml chicken stock
100g Stilton cheese
500g puff pastry
egg wash, made with
    1 egg yolk and
    1 tablespoon milk

*You will also need four
    individual pie dishes,
    about 300ml in capacity*

Slice the pork into roughly 2 to 3cm pieces and place in a bowl with the thyme, port, garlic and cranberries and season with salt and pepper. Give everything a good stir around and leave to marinate for up to 2 hours. If, however, you are reading this recipe at the last minute, which is quite possibly the case, then the pork will be fine without any marinating, the flavour just won't be as rich.

Preheat the oven to 200°C/fan 180°C/gas 6.

Drain the marinated pork in a colander over a bowl. Heat the oil in a large frying or sauté pan and cook the onion for about 5 minutes until it is softened. Stir in the mushrooms and fry for a minute before adding the drained pork and cranberries and cooking for 2 to 3 minutes. Stir in the reserved marinating liquid, bring to a simmer and then add the cream and stock. Simmer for 15 minutes. Stir in the Stilton until it has melted and remove from the heat.

Spoon the creamy pork into the pie dishes. Roll out the pastry on a lightly floured surface so it is just big enough to cut out four tops slightly bigger than the pie dishes. Brush around the rims of the dishes with the egg wash, sit the pastry on top and brush the surface with egg wash. Press around the edges to seal and cut a slit in the top for steam to escape.

Sit the pies on a baking tray and bake for 25 to 30 minutes until the tops are golden. The pastry might fall into the dishes slightly, which is fine.

**PS . . .** As well as the Root Vegetable and Mustard Mash, the pies are delicious served with some cooked green beans tossed in butter and a good pinch of garlic salt.

# ROOT VEGETABLE AND MUSTARD MASH

Making a mash with a selection of root vegetables is a great way of using up the odd vegetable sitting in the fridge. The addition of wholegrain mustard gives a mild, tasty flavour, but can easily be left out or replaced with slightly stronger Dijon or English mustard. You can even use a selection of chopped herbs.

• SERVES 4  • 30 MINUTES

900g–1.2kg mixed root
   vegetables, such as
   parsnips, swede, sweet
   potatoes, potatoes
   and carrots

50g butter

sea salt and freshly
   ground black pepper

2 teaspoons wholegrain
   mustard

Peel and chop the vegetables to roughly the same-sized chunks. Place in a pan of salted water and bring to the boil. Cook the vegetables until they are tender (about 20 minutes) and then drain well.

Return the vegetables to the pan and allow the steam to evaporate for a minute before mashing with the butter, seasoning and mustard.

Serve while piping hot.

# TOASTED CIABATTA WITH ROASTED GARLIC

When whole bulbs of garlic are roasted, they become wonderfully soft, mellow and sticky, making them perfect to squeeze out and spread on to some toasted ciabatta. Try dipping the toasted ciabatta into olive oil and balsamic vinegar for added flavour.

• SERVES 4 TO 6  • 10 MINUTES, PLUS ABOUT 45 MINUTES COOKING

2 bulbs of garlic
olive oil, for drizzling
1–2 loaves of ciabatta
extra-virgin olive oil,
  for dipping
balsamic vinegar,
  for dipping

Preheat the oven to 200°C/fan 180°C/gas 6.

Cut the tops off the garlic, just low enough to remove the tips of the individual cloves. Drizzle with a little olive oil and wrap in a double layer of aluminium foil. Place on a baking tray and roast in the oven for 45 minutes or until they feel soft when lightly pressed.

The ciabatta can just be heated through in the oven, but it is really nice to add a slightly smoky flavour by toasting it on a griddle pan. Slice in half lengthways, drizzle lightly with olive oil and place on a hot griddle pan for a minute or so each side until you have deeply golden griddle lines. You might need to press the bread down on to the griddle for even cooking.

Cut the ciabatta into pieces or leave whole to tear off yourself. Serve with the roasted garlic on the side, ready to squeeze and spread on top, and little bowls of extra-virgin olive oil and balsamic vinegar for dipping.

**PS . . .** You can make a larger quantity of roasted garlic and keep it in an airtight container in the fridge for up to a week. It is delicious stirred into gravies, dressings, soups, mayonnaise or hummus, added to cooked veg or mashed potato or tossed into pasta with some cream, Parmesan and fried pancetta.

# STEAK NIGHT

Steak is one of the simplest things to cook. It's delicious with a dollop of mustard on the side, but to really show off, why not serve it with a selection of flavoured butters? These are best made in advance, giving them time to chill. They'll keep in the fridge for a couple of weeks or, for those Boy Scouts out there who like to be prepared, you could freeze them and they'll last for months, ready and waiting for that boys' night in.

• EACH BUTTER EASILY MAKES ENOUGH FOR 6 TO 8 STEAKS

175g good-quality lightly salted butter,
    at room temperature
6–8 steaks (see PS . . . )
olive oil
sea salt and freshly ground black pepper
Beer-battered Onion Rings (see page 107)
watercress and/or grilled tomato halves,
    to serve

plus your choice of the following:

*Wild Mushroom,*
    *Thyme and Garlic Butter*
25g dried wild mushrooms,
    soaked in hot water for 30 minutes,
    then drained really well
2 cloves of garlic, crushed
2 teaspoons thyme leaves

*Béarnaise Butter*
leaves from a 10g bunch of tarragon
1 small shallot, roughly chopped
1 teaspoon white wine vinegar
a pinch of cayenne pepper
a squeeze of lemon juice
a few good twists of black pepper

*Anchovy, Garlic and Parsley Butter*
25g anchovy fillets in oil,
    drained and roughly chopped
2 cloves of garlic, crushed
2 tablespoons chopped parsley

*Au Poivre Butter*
3 tablespoons green peppercorns in brine,
    drained
1 tablespoon brandy
1 teaspoon Worcestershire sauce
1 tablespoon Dijon mustard
1 small shallot, peeled and roughly chopped

*Stilton and Watercress Butter*
50g mature Stilton, crumbled
50g watercress

*Red Wine and Mustard Butter*
100ml red wine, boiled until reduced
    to 3 tablespoons, then cooled
2 tablespoons Dijon mustard
1 tablespoon chopped parsley

To make the butters, place the ingredients for whichever you are making in a food processor and blend. Spoon the flavoured butter on to a square of clingfilm, roll the clingfilm around the butter to form a sausage shape about 3cm in diameter, then twist the ends to seal. Keep in the fridge or freezer until needed. When you are ready to serve the butter, cut into thick slices.

To cook your steaks, heat a griddle or non-stick frying pan until it is super hot, but not smoking. Rub or brush the steaks with a drop of oil and season with salt and a little pepper.

If there is a layer of fat on any steak, use a pair of tongs to hold the steak, place in the pan fat-side down and cook briefly for the fat to become golden.

Now, lay the steaks flat in the pan and sear quickly for up to a minute each side before lowering the heat and cooking for between 2 to 3 minutes each side for medium-rare. Obviously, add or take away a minute or so for more or less well-done steaks.

Remove the steak from the pan, sit it on a warm plate and leave it to rest for a good few minutes (this is essential) before serving with a couple of slices of butter on top, which will deliciously melt over the steak.

Serve with onion rings and the watercress and/or grilled tomatoes.

**PS . . .** Which steak?

**The choice about which steak you use is entirely up to you. If you are unsure about the differences, here is a guide:**

*Fillet* Very tender, but the lack of fat makes it less flavoursome. Can be quite expensive.

*Rib-eye* Perhaps the most flavoursome due to the strips of fat running through it.

*Rump* Not as tender as other steaks, but very juicy and tasty.

*Sirloin* Lovely flavour and a relatively tender cut, with a strip of flavoursome fat on the edge.

**PPS . . .** The butters are also great served with pan-fried or grilled fish.

# BEER-BATTERED ONION RINGS

What better accompaniment to the steaks could you ask for?

• SERVES 4 TO 6   • 20 MINUTES

2 large onions

2 tablespoons plain flour

sea salt and freshly ground
   black pepper

100g self-raising flour

1 egg, separated

150ml cold lager

about 1 litre groundnut
   or sunflower oil, for frying

Peel the onions and slice into rings up to 1cm thick. Separate individual rings and take out the smaller insides to the onions. These can be kept to chop for another recipe.

Place the plain flour in a medium-sized sandwich bag or bowl and season with salt and pepper. Toss the onion rings in the flour to coat.

Place the self-raising flour in a large bowl and make a well in the middle. Add the egg yolk, and then whisk in the lager to form a smooth batter.

In a separate bowl, whisk the egg white until it forms soft peaks and then fold into the batter.

Pour enough oil into a large wok to fill it by a third to a half and heat to about 180ºC. You can test the temperature by dropping in a cube of bread. It should become golden in about 20 seconds.

Line a large plate with kitchen paper ready to drain the excess oil off the onion rings. Dip the flour-coated rings, a few at a time, into the batter and then deep-fry for about 3 to 4 minutes until they are golden and crispy. Drain on the kitchen paper while you make the rest. Season with sea salt and serve.

# HALF-POUNDER GREEK LAMB BURGERS (ONE FOR THE BARBIE)

Barbecues – the ultimate boys' toy. You'll be as proud as punch cooking home-made burgers for your boys' night in. However, take it from me, blackened burgers are 'orrible. Be patient, let the BBQ reach a white heat, then cook the burgers until they're nice and golden.

• MAKES 6 HALF-POUND BURGERS  • 45 MINUTES

### for the burgers

1kg lamb mince (don't use extra-lean mince for burgers, because the fat will keep the burgers moist and add flavour)

3 cloves of garlic, chopped

1 red onion, finely chopped

2 tablespoons tomato purée

1 egg, lightly beaten

50g fresh white breadcrumbs

3 tablespoons finely chopped black kalamata olives

100g feta cheese, finely crumbled

1 teaspoon ground cumin

1 teaspoon ground coriander

2 tablespoons chopped fresh oregano or 2 teaspoons dried oregano

sea salt and freshly ground black pepper

6 burger buns, flat breads or pitta breads

To prepare the burgers, place everything except the burger buns in a large bowl and mix until thoroughly combined. I find it best to squish everything together using my hands. Yes, it's messy, but it's far quicker.

Shape the mixture into six burgers, or, if you want quarter-pounders, make twelve. Place in the fridge for half an hour or so to firm up if you have the time.

To make the tzatziki, place all of the ingredients in a food processor or blender and whizz together until you have a creamy consistency. Season to taste.

For a salad to serve alongside, roughly chop the tomatoes, cucumber, red onion and parsley. Mix together with the black olives, lemon juice and olive oil and season with salt and pepper.

When you're ready to cook the burgers, make sure the barbecue is nice and hot (the coals should be glowing white). Brush the rack with a little olive oil and cook the burgers for about 8 minutes, turning them every minute or so.

Once the burgers are cooked, heat or toast the bread on the barbecue and serve with the burgers, tzatziki and salad.

**PS . . .** If you're interested in trying some other flavours for the burgers, have a go at the ones opposite.

*for the feta tzatziki*

100g feta cheese, crumbled

150g thick Greek yoghurt

4cm piece of cucumber,
    roughly chopped

a handful of mint leaves

1 clove of garlic, crushed

sea salt and freshly ground
    black pepper

*for the Greek salad*

4 ripe tomatoes

½ cucumber

1 small red onion

1 bunch of flat-leaf parsley

a couple of handfuls
    of pitted black
    kalamata olives

a good squeeze
    of lemon juice

a good glug of extra-virgin
    olive oil

sea salt and freshly ground
    black pepper

## Indian-spiced Burgers

Swap the chopped olives for 2 tablespoons mango chutney; omit the feta; replace the oregano with coriander and add 1 chopped red chilli, 2cm peeled, chopped ginger and ½ teaspoon ground turmeric. Serve with mini naan breads, the same salad (minus the olives) and call the Feta Tzatziki, Feta Raita!

## Chilli con Carne Burgers

Use beef mince rather than the lamb; swap the feta and olives for a 400g tin of drained kidney beans; use coriander instead of the oregano and add 1 tablespoon cocoa powder and 2 chopped red chillies. Serve with guacamole, sour cream, wedges of lime and tortilla breads.

# TOMATO SPICED MUSSELS AND SPAGHETTI

This is a really tasty dish and wonderfully easy to make. If you fancy a bit on the side, serve with some crusty bread to mop up the delicious juices or you could make the Toasted Ciabatta with Roasted Garlic (see page 103).

• SERVES 4   • 20 MINUTES

1.5kg mussels

3 tablespoons olive oil

1 long red chilli, chopped (deseeded for a less spicy flavour)

4 plump cloves of garlic, chopped

1 red onion, finely chopped

½ medium fennel, very finely chopped

500g dried spaghetti

200ml white wine

400g tin of chopped tomatoes

sea salt and freshly ground black pepper

3 tablespoons chopped flat-leaf parsley

Wash the mussels in cold water, pulling off any straggly beards. Throw away any that remain open after a few seconds when lightly tapped.

Heat a large lidded saucepan and add the oil. Sauté the chilli, garlic, onion and fennel and cook gently for a good 15 minutes until everything is nicely softened.

Meanwhile, cook the spaghetti until al dente.

Stir the wine, chopped tomatoes and some salt and pepper into the large pan and cook for 5 minutes. Increase the heat and then add the mussels and parsley. Give them a good stir around, cover with a lid and cook for 3 to 4 minutes. By then, the mussels will be cooked.

Using a large slotted spoon, remove the mussels, putting them in a large bowl or a saucepan, and add the cooked, drained spaghetti to the sauce. Toss around until coated and divide among four serving bowls. Spoon the mussels on top, discarding any that haven't opened.

Serve straight away, with a separate bowl for the discarded mussel shells.

# WHISKY BREAD-AND-BUTTER PUDDING

This is a real man's pudding. It has a slight twist on the classic bread-and-butter pudding because it's flavoured with sultanas soaked in whisky and a hint of marmalade.

• SERVES 6 TO 8   • 45 MINUTES, PLUS 20 TO 30 MINUTES STANDING AND SOAKING OVERNIGHT

125g sultanas

5 tablespoons whisky

50g butter,
   at room temperature

12 medium slices
   of white bread

3 tablespoons marmalade

2 whole eggs

4 egg yolks

150g caster sugar,
   plus 4 tablespoons
   extra for glazing

400ml milk

400ml double cream

1 teaspoon vanilla extract

*You will also need a
   1.5–1.8-litre baking dish
   greased with butter and
   a large piece of buttered
   foil*

Cover the sultanas with the whisky and leave to soak overnight (if you don't have that long, then see the PS . . . ).

Butter the bread, remove the crusts and then cut each piece diagonally in half. Spread the marmalade on the bottom of the buttered dish. Arrange the bread in the dish in overlapping layers, sprinkling the whisky-soaked sultanas in between and reserving any leftover whisky.

Preheat the oven to 160°C/fan 140°C/gas 3.

In a large bowl, beat together the whole eggs, egg yolks and 150g caster sugar until creamy. Add the milk, cream, vanilla and any remaining whisky. Slowly pour this over the bread, pressing down so the slices are submerged. Leave to stand for about 20 to 30 minutes for the custard to soak into the bread.

Stand the bread-and-butter-pudding dish in a large roasting tray filled with enough boiling water to come halfway up the sides of the dish. Cover with the buttered foil and place in the oven for 30 minutes until the pudding is just beginning to set when you press lightly in the centre.

Remove from the roasting tray and leave to rest for about 10 minutes for the pudding to continue setting, before sprinkling the top with the 4 tablespoons of caster sugar.

Now for the best bit. Glaze the top of the pudding by slowly moving a blowtorch back and forth over the top until the sugar caramelizes to a deep golden colour. Alternatively, you can place it under a very hot grill until golden.

**PS . . .** If you don't have time to soak the sultanas overnight, you can place them in a small saucepan with the whisky and heat gently until they are piping hot. Leave to soak for about 1 hour.

# SIMPLE FRIDAY NIGHT SUPPERS

*'TFI Friday,' I hear you say. I've kept it simple and I've made it beautiful. All the dishes are the perfect way to end the week, especially the Pork and Porcini Stroganoff with the Red Pepper Braised Wild Rice. They knock spots off any takeaway, so don't even think about it.*

*PS . . . I know beetroot has been used twice – that's because I love it.*

# Menu

### Spring/Summer Fish Supper Menu

Smoked Mackerel and Horseradish Fishcakes
 with Avocado, Beetroot and Caper Salsa

Blackberry and Lemon Curd Fool

### Spring/Summer Quick-cook Menu

Saffron and Pesto Spaghetti
 with Beetroot and Feta

Pimm's and Strawberry Ripple Creams

### Autumn/Winter Make-ahead Menu

Baked Fish and Prawn Lasagne

Chocolate, Mascarpone and Raspberry Tarts

### Autumn/Winter Stress-free Menu

Pork and Porcini Stroganoff
 with Red Pepper Braised Wild Rice

Pear and Pecan Tarts
 with Speedy Banoffee Ice-cream

# SMOKED MACKEREL AND HORSERADISH FISHCAKES WITH AVOCADO, BEETROOT AND CAPER SALSA

The mild, smoky flavour of the mackerel used in these fishcakes is a very tasty, and far quicker, alternative to traditional fishcakes made from salmon or cod, which needs cooking first. They can be prepared the day before or even frozen. Use the fresh beetroot in mild vinegar from the salad section of the supermarket if you can.

• SERVES 4        • 45 MINUTES TO MAKE, PLUS 30 MINUTES CHILLING

500g medium potatoes, peeled and halved

3 tablespoons hot horseradish sauce

500g smoked mackerel fillets

1 bunch of spring onions, finely chopped

1 tablespoon chopped tarragon

grated zest of 1 lemon

freshly ground black pepper

8 tablespoons semolina

sunflower or vegetable oil, for frying

*for the salsa*

2 tablespoons sunflower seeds

200g cooked beetroot, cut into small cubes

½ red onion, finely chopped

2 tablespoons capers, roughly chopped

1 tablespoon chopped parsley

1 tablespoon extra-virgin olive oil

sea salt and freshly ground black pepper

1 ripe avocado

Cook the potatoes in boiling salted water until they are cooked through, then drain and mash with the horseradish sauce.

Peel away the skin from the mackerel and flake the fillets into the potato, removing any bones. Add the spring onions, tarragon, lemon zest and season with black pepper. You shouldn't need any salt as the mackerel is naturally salty.

Gently bind everything together and shape the mixture into four large or eight smaller cakes. Do this with wet hands so the mixture doesn't stick to you.

Put the fishcakes in the fridge for about 30 minutes or more to firm up, but they can be cooked straight away if necessary.

For the salsa, lightly toast the sunflower seeds in a small dry frying pan until just golden and crunchy. Leave to cool.

Place the beetroot in a mixing bowl with the red onion, capers, chopped parsley and olive oil. Season and keep to one side until needed.

Just before serving, peel and chop the avocado into chunks about the size of the beetroot and stir into the salsa with the sunflower seeds.

Sprinkle the semolina on a plate or shallow dish and lightly coat the surface of each fishcake.

Heat about 1cm of oil in a large frying pan over a low to medium heat. Fry the fishcakes for 3 to 4 minutes each side until golden, crispy and heated through. You will most likely have to do this in a couple of batches.

Remove the cooked fishcakes from the frying pan, sit them on kitchen paper to absorb any excess oil and keep them warm in a low oven while you cook the rest.

Serve straight away with the Avocado, Beetroot and Caper Salsa, a dollop of sour cream or crème fraîche and greenery of your choice.

# BLACKBERRY AND LEMON CURD FOOL

I'm a bit of a lemon curd fan and love to use it when I can as a short cut ingredient for desserts. In this rather indulgent fool, it adds a delicious sweet lemon flavour (funnily enough), which works really well with the slight tartness of the blackberries.

• SERVES 4 • 10 MINUTES, PLUS 1 ½ HOURS COOLING/CHILLING

250g blackberries
50g caster sugar
2 tablespoons crème de cassis
200ml double cream
200g Greek yoghurt
200g good-quality lemon curd
mint sprigs, for garnish
small dessert biscuits or
   shortbread to serve
   (optional)

Place 200g of the blackberries, the sugar and crème de cassis in a small saucepan and cook for about 5 minutes until the blackberries have become mushy. Blend to a purée and strain through a sieve. Leave for about 30 minutes to cool completely.

Whip the cream until it forms soft peaks. In a separate bowl, mix together the Greek yoghurt and lemon curd. Stir this into the cream, then gently fold in the cooled blackberry purée, leaving the fool with a swirly finish or folding the purée in completely. Spoon into individual glasses or dishes and place in the fridge for at least 1 hour to chill.

When you are ready to serve, garnish with the remaining blackberries and mint. Serve with the biscuits if you wish.

PS . . . The blackberries can be swapped with raspberries, blueberries or strawberries for a different flavour, using matching fruit liqueurs or simply sticking with the crème de cassis.

# SAFFRON AND PESTO SPAGHETTI WITH BEETROOT AND FETA

Pasta is always a winner when it comes to wanting something fast and that is exactly what this is (as well as being rather delicious and exceptionally colourful). Try to avoid using pickled beetroot if you can, because you'll find the vinegar flavour is a little too strong and overpowering. It's best to use the packs of fresh beetroot in mild vinegar sold in the salad section of the supermarket.

• SERVES 4   • 20 MINUTES

a large pinch of saffron

500g dried spaghetti

2 tablespoons olive oil

3 large shallots,
   thinly sliced

300g cooked beetroot,
   cut into small cubes

sea salt and freshly ground
   black pepper

4 tablespoons good-quality
   bought pesto

400g feta cheese, crumbled

Place the saffron in a small dish with 3 tablespoons boiling water and leave to infuse while you cook the pasta.

Cook the spaghetti until al dente.

While the pasta is cooking, heat the olive oil in a saucepan and lightly sauté the shallots until they are softened and just taking on a light golden colour. Add the beetroot, cooking until it is heated through. Season well.

Drain the pasta well, return to the pan and toss with the saffron water, pesto and seasoning. Stir in the feta and divide among four dishes. Spoon the warm beetroot on top. Serve straight away.

**PS . . .** If you are using freshly cooked beetroot that doesn't have any vinegar at all, it is worth adding 1 tablespoon balsamic vinegar to the pan with the beetroot.

# PIMM'S AND STRAWBERRY RIPPLE CREAMS

You can't go wrong with this super-quick dessert for a warm Friday evening supper. They look very elegant served in individual glasses and the flavours just shout 'Summer!' As an alternative to meringue, biscotti biscuits are also very nice.

• SERVES 4   • 10 MINUTES

3 tablespoons caster sugar

50ml Pimm's

grated zest of 1 large orange

275ml double cream

225–250g strawberries, sliced

175–200ml strawberry sauce, bought or home-made (see PS . . . )

3 individual meringues, bought or home-made, crushed into smallish chunks

6 sprigs of mint (optional)

In a large bowl, stir the caster sugar into the Pimm's until it starts to dissolve. Add the orange zest and double cream and whisk manually or with an electric hand whisk (which is far easier and quicker) until it is thick enough to just hold its shape.

Take four glass dishes, sundae glasses or wine glasses and randomly layer up the strawberries, Pimm's cream, strawberry sauce and crumbled meringue to create a ripple effect. Finish by garnishing with a sprig of mint, if using. Keep in the fridge until needed or serve straight away.

PS . . . To make your own strawberry sauce, blend together 200g strawberries with about 50g caster or icing sugar (more or less will be needed depending on the sweetness of your strawberries) until you have a smooth purée.

# BAKED FISH AND PRAWN LASAGNE

This very tasty alternative to fish pie makes a great Friday night fish supper. Please don't be put off by the long list of ingredients. It is really straightforward to make and can easily be put together the day before and kept in the fridge, ready to bake when needed. There'll be plenty to serve four hungry people with a big bowl of salad or it will easily stretch to six if you serve some nice Italian bread on the side.

• SERVES 4 TO 6   • 40 MINUTES, PLUS 45 MINUTES IN THE OVEN

75g butter

1 onion, finely chopped

½ fennel bulb, finely chopped

2 sticks of celery, thinly sliced

2 bay leaves

450ml passata

3 tablespoons finely sliced basil leaves

2 tablespoons olive oil

sea salt and freshly ground black pepper

75g plain flour

250ml white wine

a small pinch of saffron

400ml fish stock

150ml double cream

700g fish fillets (try a selection of salmon, monkfish and cod, haddock or pollock)

a small bunch of flat-leaf parsley, chopped

200g raw peeled prawns

9–12 dried no-cook lasagne verde sheets

40g Parmesan cheese, grated

*You will also need a large (about 2 litre) ovenproof lasagne dish.*

Preheat the oven to 180°C/fan 160°C/gas 4.

Melt the butter in a large non-stick saucepan. Add the onion, fennel, celery and bay leaves and cook with the lid on for 10 minutes.

Meanwhile, to make the tomato sauce, simply mix together the passata, basil and olive oil and season with salt and pepper.

Stir the flour into the onion mixture and, after a minute of cooking, add the white wine and saffron. Stir to a smooth paste before adding the stock and double cream. Bring the sauce to a simmer, stirring occasionally, and cook for 5 minutes.

Remove any skin from the fish and cut into chunks. Add to the creamy sauce with the parsley and prawns and cook for a few minutes, stirring gently a couple of times. Season with salt and pepper.

Spoon a third of the creamy fish sauce into the bottom of your dish, spreading it into the corners, followed by a layer of lasagne sheets, then just a thin layer of the tomato sauce. Repeat this twice, with the creamy fish sauce, lasagne and tomato sauce, making the final tomato sauce a nice generous layer. Scatter the Parmesan over the top and sit the dish on a baking tray.

Bake in the oven for about 45 minutes until it is bubbling. Leave to cool down for 5 to 10 minutes before serving.

**PS . . .** A couple of tablespoons of small capers are a nice addition to the tomato sauce, and for an extra fish flavour, you can lay a few anchovies on top of the lasagne before baking.

# CHOCOLATE, MASCARPONE AND RASPBERRY TARTS

Tart is possibly the wrong word for these divine chocolate treats. They are more like a rich, dense sponge cooked in the shape of a tart. Nevertheless, you'll love them. The raspberries prevent them from being too rich and the sweet mascarpone swirled through adds a soft creaminess.

• MAKES 6   • 30 MINUTES, PLUS 20 MINUTES IN THE OVEN

125g butter
50g cocoa powder
75g raspberry jam
150g caster sugar
2 eggs, plus 1 egg yolk
100g plain flour
½ teaspoon baking powder
125g mascarpone cheese
150g raspberries
crème fraîche or whipped
  cream, to serve (optional)
icing sugar or cocoa powder,
  to dust

*You will also need six
  10cm x 3cm deep
  loose-bottomed tart tins,
  greased with melted butter*

Preheat the oven to 180°C/fan 160°C/gas 4.

Melt the butter in a medium-sized saucepan over a low heat and sift in the cocoa powder. Stir until the mixture boils, then remove from the heat. Stir in the jam, 100g of the caster sugar, the whole eggs (not the separate yolk), flour and baking powder.

Divide the mixture among the tart tins and keep to one side.

Beat together the mascarpone cheese, egg yolk and the remaining 50g of caster sugar and place a spoonful in the middle of each tart. Pull a knife backwards and forwards a few times to create a marbled effect, and then push the raspberries into the mixture, dividing them equally among the six tarts.

Place on a baking tray and bake for 20 minutes until the tarts have risen and are just firm to the touch.

Remove from the tins after they have cooled for a few minutes and serve warm or cold with cream and a light dusting of icing sugar or cocoa powder.

**PS . . .** If you are cooking for four, then the two tarts that are left over will freeze really well (or just tuck in to them the next day).

# PORK AND PORCINI STROGANOFF WITH RED PEPPER BRAISED WILD RICE

Make sure you have done all your chopping and preparation before you start adding things to the frying pan.

• SERVES 4   • 35 MINUTES, PLUS 30 MINUTES SOAKING FOR THE MUSHROOMS

40g dried porcini mushrooms
1 tablespoon olive oil
1 onion, thinly sliced
2 cloves of garlic, crushed
750g pork fillet,
    cut into slim strips
a pinch of cayenne pepper
1 teaspoon paprika
3 tablespoons brandy
1 teaspoon Dijon mustard
200ml sour cream
    or crème fraîche
150ml chicken stock or water
a squeeze of lemon juice
sea salt and freshly ground
    black pepper
1 tablespoon chopped parsley

### for the rice
40g butter
1 large onion, chopped
2 cloves of garlic, crushed
2 red peppers, finely chopped
1 bay leaf
250g basmati and wild rice
500ml vegetable
    or chicken stock
sea salt and freshly ground
    black pepper
150g baby spinach leaves

Cover the porcini mushrooms with at least 300ml hot water and leave to soak for about 30 minutes.

For the rice, preheat the oven to 170°C/fan 150°C/gas 3–4. Melt the butter in a heavy-bottomed braising or casserole pan with a lid. Sauté the onion, garlic and red peppers for about 10 minutes until softened but not coloured.

Add the bay leaf and rice and cook for a further minute before adding the stock and seasoning. Bring to the boil and cover with the lid. Place in the oven for 20 minutes. Leave to stand with the lid on for a few minutes. You can also leave the rice for up to 30 minutes in the oven with the heat turned off and it will stay hot.

Heat a large frying pan with a drop of olive oil and gently sauté the onion for about 5 minutes. Add the garlic and pork, frying for a couple of minutes.

Strain the mushrooms, reserving 200ml of the liquid, and add the mushrooms to the pan. Cook for a couple of minutes before stirring in the cayenne and paprika, then pour in the brandy, allowing it to flambé to burn off the alcohol. This is easy with a gas flame because all you need to do is tilt the pan towards the flame. If you are using an electric hob, hold a lit match to one edge of the pan and it will flambé.

Stir in the mustard, sour cream, reserved porcini liquid and chicken stock or water. Bring to a simmer, cook for 5 minutes or so, then squeeze in the lemon juice, season and scatter with parsley. Stir the spinach into the rice and serve straight away.

PS . . . A word of warning: when you flambé the stroganoff, switch your extractor fan off because it will suck the flames up. Unfortunately, I'm talking from experience!

# PEAR AND PECAN TARTS
# WITH SPEEDY BANOFFEE ICE-CREAM

Home-made ice-cream in minutes? Oh yes, it's possible and, what's more, it's so-o-o delicious.

• MAKES 6   • 20 MINUTES, PLUS 2 HOURS FREEZING

### for the ice-cream

4 bananas, cut into smallish chunks

150ml fresh ready-made custard

75ml double cream

4 tablespoons bought toffee sauce (dulce de leche)

### for the tarts

6 tinned pear halves, drained

375g ready-rolled puff pastry

2–3 tablespoons bought toffee sauce (dulce de leche)

1 egg, beaten

75g pecan nuts, broken in half

icing sugar, for dusting

Freeze the chopped bananas in a sealed plastic sandwich bag for about 2 hours, until completely frozen through. This can be done days in advance.

Preheat the oven to 200°C/fan 180°C/gas 6.

For the tarts, slice each pear into three wedges and pat dry with kitchen paper.

Cut the pastry into six circles about 10cm in diameter. Place on a lightly greased baking tray and score a small border of about 5mm to 1cm around the inside edge of each one.

Put about 1 teaspoon of toffee sauce in the centre of each piece of pastry and then arrange the pear slices on top. Brush the top of the pears and the pastry edges with the egg, scatter over the pecans and then dust each one fairly generously with icing sugar.

Place in the oven for 12 to 15 minutes until the pastry is puffed up and golden around the edges.

Literally just before serving, place the frozen bananas in a food processor with the custard, double cream and toffee sauce. Blitz until you have a smooth ice-cream and serve straight away with the tarts.

# SUNDAY LUNCH
# THREE WAYS

*Sunday lunch conjures up some wonderful memories for me. Family get-togethers, long afternoons in a country pub, being so full that I can't move and afternoon naps – if only every day was a Sunday.*

# Menu

## Traditional with a Twist Menu

Peppered Roast Beef
with Roast Onions and
Rich Red Wine Gravy

Wild Mushroom Yorkies

Honey Roast Veg and Garlic

Mustard Buttered Greens

Cherry Pie with Chocolate Pastry

## Prepare-ahead Menu

Italian Braised Lamb Shanks
with Crispy Parmesan Crumbs

Easy Peach Melba Cheesecake

## Quick-cook Menu

Lazy Tray-baked Chicken

Plum, Apple and Almond Crumble
with Amaretto Cream

# PEPPERED ROAST BEEF WITH ROAST ONIONS AND RICH RED WINE GRAVY

If you love a traditional Sunday roast but need some inspiration to liven it up a little. then read on.

• SERVES 6 • 15 MINUTES, PLUS 40 MINUTES TO 1 HOUR 10 MINUTES ROASTING

1–2 tablespoons olive oil

sea salt

about 1.2–1.5kg boned rib of beef

1 tablespoon Dijon mustard

2 teaspoons coarsely ground black pepper

2 tablespoons demerara sugar

4 onions, peeled and cut into 1cm-thick round slices

2–3 sprigs of thyme

*for the gravy*

1 tablespoon plain flour

2 tablespoons tomato purée

2–3 sprigs of thyme

350ml full-bodied red wine

400ml mushroom soaking liquid from the Wild Mushroom Yorkies recipe (see page 136) or beef stock

1 tablespoon demerara sugar

sea salt and freshly ground black pepper

Preheat the oven to 200°C/fan 180°C/gas 6.

Heat the oil in a sturdy roasting tray on the hob. Rub plenty of salt over the beef. Spread the mustard over the surface and then press the pepper and demerara over the top so they cling on to the mustard.

Brown the beef on all sides in the hot oil. Remove from the pan, add the onion and thyme and then sit the beef on top. Drizzle the onion with a little oil and place in the oven to roast, allowing 15 minutes per 450g for rare or 20 minutes per 450g for medium.

While the beef is cooking, make the Wild Mushroom Yorkies batter (see page 136) and leave to rest. The Honey Roast Veg and Garlic (see page 139) can also be put into the oven while the beef is cooking.

Once the beef is cooked, transfer to a plate, cover loosely with foil and keep in a warm place to rest while you cook the yorkies and gravy.

To make the gravy, pour away any excess fat from the beef roasting tray. Place the tray over a high heat on the hob and stir in the flour and tomato purée. Add the thyme and red wine. Boil for a few minutes until the wine has reduced in quantity by about a third. Pour in the stock and sugar and simmer gently for about 5 minutes. Strain through a sieve and season if needed.

The juicy and slightly caramelized roasted onions can also be transferred to a plate and kept hot, ready to serve as a vegetable accompaniment.

# WILD MUSHROOM YORKIES

• MAKES 12   • 30 MINUTES, PLUS 30 MINUTES SOAKING AND 30 MINUTES RESTING

15g dried mixed
  wild mushrooms

225g plain flour

a pinch of salt

1 teaspoon dried thyme

3 eggs, beaten

1 egg white

300–400ml milk

about 4 tablespoons
  beef dripping, goose fat,
  groundnut or vegetable oil,
  for cooking

*You will also need a*
  *twelve-hole deep muffin tin*

Cover the mushrooms with hot water and leave to soak for about 30 minutes.

Sift the flour and salt into a mixing bowl, add the thyme and whisk in the beaten eggs, egg white and enough of the milk to give a smooth thick batter about the consistency of double cream.

If you can, leave the batter to rest for about 30 minutes.

Drain the mushrooms from the water, reserving the liquid to use in the gravy. Squeeze out as much liquid as you can from the mushrooms and then chop them very finely. Whisk into the batter.

Increase the heat of the oven to 220°C/fan 200°C/gas 8.

Pour about 1 teaspoon of the beef dripping or oil into each hole of the muffin tin and place in the oven for a few minutes until the oil is almost smoking.

As soon as you take the tray out of the oven, pour or ladle the batter into the holes, three-quarters filling each one. Immediately place back into the oven and cook for about 25 to 30 minutes, until they are golden and crispy.

# HONEY ROAST VEG AND GARLIC

• SERVES 6 • 10 MINUTES, PLUS 45 TO 55 MINUTES ROASTING

4 medium-large carrots
2 large sweet potatoes
1 celeriac
3–4 medium beetroot
1 bulb of garlic
3 tablespoons olive oil
sea salt and freshly ground
  black pepper
3 tablespoons runny honey

Preheat the oven to 220°C/fan 200°C/gas 8.

Peel the vegetables and cut the carrots, sweet potatoes and celeriac into 3 to 5cm chunks or wedges. The beetroot can be cut into four to six wedges each.

Place the vegetables in a roasting tray in a single layer. Scatter over the individual cloves of garlic, still with their skins on, and toss everything in the olive oil. Season with salt and pepper.

Roast in the oven with the beef for about 25 minutes. Remove from the oven and drizzle over the honey. Turn the vegetables so they are coated and return to the oven for a further 20 to 30 minutes until they are tender, sticky and golden. Serve straight away.

# MUSTARD BUTTERED GREENS

• SERVES 6 • 10 MINUTES

about 300g curly kale, spring
  greens or savoy cabbage
50g butter
1 clove of garlic, chopped
1 tablespoon Dijon or
  wholegrain mustard
sea salt and freshly ground
  black pepper

Wash and roughly chop the greens, removing any tough stalks.

Melt the butter in a large frying or sauté pan and gently cook the garlic for about 30 seconds. Increase the heat, add the greens and toss around or stir-fry for about 5 minutes until they are becoming tender.

Add a couple of tablespoons of water and the mustard and continue to cook for a further minute or two. Season with salt and pepper and serve.

# CHERRY PIE WITH CHOCOLATE PASTRY

Sunday lunch isn't complete without a fruit pie for pud.

• SERVES 4 EASILY   • 55 MINUTES, PLUS 35–40 MINUTES IN THE OVEN

*for the pastry*
175g plain flour
25g cocoa powder
100g chilled butter
4 tablespoons caster sugar
3–4 tablespoons milk
1 egg yolk, to glaze
1 tablespoon caster sugar

*for the filling*
750g fresh cherries
2 tablespoons Kirsch
   (cherry liqueur)
4 tablespoons caster sugar
1 tablespoon arrowroot

*You will also need
   a pie plate*

To make the pastry, sift the flour and cocoa powder into a food processor and blitz with the butter to form fine crumbs. Add the 4 tablespoons of sugar and then gradually add enough of the milk, processing briefly, to form a soft dough. Wrap the dough in clingfilm and chill for 30 minutes or so.

While the pastry is chilling, remove the stones from the cherries. This is fairly time-consuming (well, about 10 minutes), but doesn't require any brain power so that makes the job far more appealing. It can be made quicker if you use a cherry/olive stoner, but this isn't necessary.

Toss the stoned cherries with the Kirsch and caster sugar and leave for about 20 minutes.

Preheat the oven to 190°C/fan 170°C/gas 5.

Mix the arrowroot with a couple of spoonfuls of the cherry juices, and then stir back into the cherries. Transfer to a pie plate or shallow pie dish. Brush the edge of the plate or dish with the egg yolk.

Roll out the pastry on a lightly floured surface to a circle just a little bigger than the pie plate and drape over the top of the cherries. Press the pastry on to the edges of the plate to seal and trim any excess. Pierce a hole in the pastry to allow steam to escape and then brush the surface with the egg yolk. Scatter with the caster sugar and place in the oven for 35 to 40 minutes until the pastry is crisp and the juices are starting to bubble over the edges of the pie plate.

Leave for 5 to 10 minutes before serving with ice-cream or custard.

**PS . . .** If fresh cherries are out of season, this works just as well using frozen cherries. Leave to defrost in a sieve to remove excess juices and continue as above. The bonus here is that there are no stones to remove because that is already done for you.

# ITALIAN BRAISED LAMB SHANKS WITH CRISPY PARMESAN CRUMBS

The fantastic thing about this recipe is that you can leave it to cook for at least 2½ hours (if not longer) without touching it, giving you plenty of time to go for a long walk, lazily read the papers or take a trip to your local. If necessary, it can even be made the day before. All you need to do is be around for the last 30 minutes to add some cannellini beans. I do, however, like to serve a green veg with this, but it is entirely up to you. Some buttered savoy cabbage or steamed broccoli will go beautifully.

• SERVES 4 HEARTILY  • 30 MINUTES, PLUS 3 HOURS COOKING

*for the crispy Parmesan crumbs*

2 tablespoons olive oil

50g white breadcrumbs (from a ciabatta, standard white loaf or baguette)

25g Parmesan, finely grated

*for the lamb shanks*

3 tablespoons olive oil

sea salt and freshly ground black pepper

4 lamb shanks

1 large onion, finely chopped

2 sticks of celery, thinly sliced

1 large carrot, finely diced

6 cloves of garlic, crushed

1 medium aubergine, finely diced

300ml red wine

500ml passata

200ml lamb or chicken stock

1 tablespoon red wine vinegar

2 bay leaves

4 stalks of rosemary

75–100g pitted black olives

2 x 400g tins of cannellini beans

It's up to you when you prepare the crispy Parmesan crumbs. They can be made a couple of days in advance if necessary. Heat the olive oil in a wok or saucepan and add the breadcrumbs. Fry for a couple of minutes until golden and crunchy. Transfer to a bowl, sprinkle over the Parmesan and toss to coat the crumbs.

Preheat the oven to 180°C/fan 160°C/gas 4.

Heat the oil in a heavy ovenproof casserole dish until very hot. Season the lamb shanks and add to the pan. Sear all over until lightly golden and then remove from the casserole on to a plate.

Reduce the heat slightly and add the onion, celery, carrot and garlic and cook for about 5 minutes until softened. Stir in the aubergine and continue to cook for a further couple of minutes.

Add the red wine, passata, stock, red wine vinegar, bay leaves, rosemary and olives. Bring to a simmer and then return the lamb shanks to the casserole, covering them as much as possible in the sauce. Cover with a lid and place in the oven for 2 to 2½ hours. (If you left it longer, it wouldn't be the end of the world: the lamb would literally be falling off the bone.)

Remove the lid and stir in the cannellini beans. Return to the oven for a final 30 minutes of cooking, minus the lid.

Serve the lamb with the crispy Parmesan crumbs scattered over the top, offering any extra at the table, with vegetables on the side if you like.

# EASY PEACH MELBA CHEESECAKE

Forget fiddling about with cake tins, cooking bases or setting creamy toppings in the fridge – this is a wonderfully easy cheesecake that you make straight on to the serving plate, so it is ready in an instant. You can top the cheesecake with whatever fruits you like, but I have given you a few suggestions to get you on your way.

• SERVES SIX TO 8 EASILY   • 30 MINUTES

*for the base*
275g biscuits, such as
   digestives or shortbread
100g butter

*for the topping*
200g mascarpone cheese
175g Greek yoghurt
50g caster sugar
100ml double cream
6 tablespoons bought or
   home-made raspberry sauce
2–3 ripe peaches, sliced
100g fresh raspberries
icing sugar, for dusting

Crush the biscuits to fine crumbs in a plastic bag with a rolling pin or in a blender. Melt the butter in a saucepan and then thoroughly mix in the biscuit crumbs.

Spoon the base mixture on to a large, flat serving plate. Using a spoon or your hands, shape and firmly press the crumbs into a thick circle, roughly 22cm x 1cm (but this will depend on the size of your plate). Put the plate in a cool place, or the fridge if it will fit, while you prepare the topping.

Mix together the mascarpone cheese, Greek yoghurt and sugar until smooth. Whisk the double cream until it forms soft peaks. Stir into the mascarpone mixture and then gently stir in the raspberry sauce, giving a raspberry ripple effect. Spoon over the top of the cheesecake base and spread lightly to cover the surface, leaving a small biscuit border.

Arrange the peaches and raspberries over the top of the cheesecake, being as random or as neat as you wish. If you're not serving the cheesecake straight away, keep in the fridge until needed.

Dust with icing sugar before serving.

**PS . . .** To make your own raspberry sauce, blend 200g raspberries with about 50g caster or icing sugar until you have a smooth purée.

*Banoffee Cheesecake* Mix some bought toffee sauce (dulce de leche) into the mascarpone and top with sliced bananas and lots of grated chocolate.

*Black Forest Cheesecake* Use bought chocolate sauce in the mascarpone and top with cherry compote, or a jar of cherries in syrup, and grated chocolate.

# LAZY TRAY-BAKED CHICKEN

You'll love the simplicity of this recipe – minimal preparation, minimal washing up, but maximum flavour. There is no need for anything else to be served with it, unless you are really missing your greens, in which case a portion of tenderstem broccoli or even a green salad would be lovely.

• SERVES 4   • 15 MINUTES, PLUS 45 MINUTES TO 1 HOUR COOKING

8 boneless and skinless
   chicken thighs

2 onions,
   each cut into 4–6 wedges

2 large carrots, cut into
   large chunks

500g new potatoes, cut in half

1 large red pepper,
   cut into chunks

8 cloves of garlic, unpeeled

4 stalks of rosemary

4 tablespoons olive oil

2 teaspoons paprika

juice of ½ lemon

1 lemon, cut into wedges

150g smoked bacon lardons
   or pancetta

sea salt and freshly ground
   black pepper

2½ tablespoons runny honey

Preheat the oven to 200°C/fan 180°C/gas 6.

Toss everything together, apart from the honey, in a roasting tray. Place on the hob over a high heat and turn the chicken and vegetables around for a couple of minutes. Arrange the chicken so it is snuggled into the vegetables and then place in the oven for 30 minutes, turning the food a couple of times.

After the 30 minutes, drizzle over the honey and cook for a further 15 to 30 minutes.

Serve two chicken thighs, lots of vegetables and plenty of the sticky juices per person on to warm plates. That is it!

# PLUM, APPLE AND ALMOND CRUMBLE WITH AMARETTO CREAM

This can be prepared and baked at the same time as the Lazy Tray-baked Chicken. It is a good idea to leave the cooked crumble resting for a good 5 minutes before serving because it will be very hot. This also gives time for the juices to thicken slightly.

• SERVES 4 GENEROUSLY  • 20 MINUTES, PLUS 40 TO 50 MINUTES COOKING

*for the filling*

600g plums, stoned
  and cut into wedges
450g eating apples, peeled,
  cored and cut into
  bite-sized chunks
25g soft brown sugar
grated zest of 1 orange
3 tablespoons apple juice

*for the topping*

125g softened unsalted
  butter
150g plain flour
1 teaspoon ground cinnamon
a pinch of salt
75g flaked almonds,
  crushed lightly
  in your hands
40g rolled oats
100g soft brown sugar

*for the cream*

275ml double cream
3 tablespoons amaretto

*You will also need an
  ovenproof dish, about
  1.5 litres in capacity*

Preheat the oven to 200°C/fan 180°C/gas 6.

To make the filling, toss the plums, apples, sugar, orange zest and apple juice together. Tip into the ovenproof dish.

For the topping, lightly rub together the butter, flour, cinnamon and salt, then stir in the almonds, oats and three-quarters of the sugar. Keep the topping fairly chunky and crumbly.

Scatter over the top of the fruit and finish by sprinkling the reserved sugar on top. Place on a baking tray and cook for 40 to 50 minutes until the topping is crisp and golden and the fruity juices are bubbling around the edges. If the topping is becoming too golden, then just cover loosely with a piece of aluminium foil. Remove from the oven and leave to cool for a good 5 minutes.

To prepare the cream, whisk the cream until it is just starting to thicken, stir in the Amaretto and continue to whisk until it forms soft peaks. Serve in a bowl for spooning on top of the crumble.

# CHAPTER THREE
## THE 'DINNER PARTY'

What a lovely idea the dinner party is. In a nutshell, you invite people round and at some point they invite you back. You get to meet new people, old friends and colleagues from work, or outside work, along with their partners (they are never as you imagined, are they?). And while you're there, you can put the world to rights and play games (why do couples often end up on the brink of divorce playing simple games?). Just don't forget to dress up, be charming and, above all, cook up some top food.

Whenever it's your turn to play host, it always seems such a good idea while the proposed date is miles off. Nearer the time, however, most people tend to panic. So I've put together some menus that will help you, whatever your situation or mood.

Please note: All these recipes have been fully tested on my friends and no one stormed out or sent anything back. Phew!

# VEGETARIAN

*My vegetarian friends are tricky customers. They can't eat meat or fish and I don't want to make something else just for them, because one, it singles them out and they feel awkward, and two, it's more washing-up. In this section you'll find a menu that doesn't include a nut roast or lentil stew which everyone will enjoy. Better still, no one will really spot that you've catered solely for your vegetarian friends.*

# Menu

*Beetroot Carpaccio
  with Herbed Ricotta*

**\*And to drink . . .**
  Although the colours of this dish are vibrant, the flavours are actually
  quite subtle, so try pairing it with a crisp, herb-scented white such as
  a Sancerre or Pouilly Fumé from France's Loire Valley.

*Roasted Red Wine Mushrooms
  with Blue Cheese and Spinach Baked Risotto*

**\*And to drink . . .**
  The rich, almost sweet character of a heady Italian Amarone
  will cope wonderfully with the salty blue cheese and the intense,
  earthy mushrooms.

*Rhubarb Marshmallow Meringue Roulade*

**\*And to drink . . .**
  The floral aromas and light,
  freshing flavour of a sparkling
  Moscato d'Asti would be
  delicious with this dish, and
  for something a bit different
  try rhubarb schnapps.

# BEETROOT CARPACCIO WITH HERBED RICOTTA

This sounds rather posh and difficult to prepare, but you'll be pleased to hear that it's not.

• SERVES 6   • 20 MINUTES

3–6 (depending on their size) whole cooked beetroot

50g walnut halves

250g ricotta cheese

100ml crème fraîche

3 tablespoons chopped chives, basil and dill

finely grated zest of ½ lemon

sea salt and freshly ground black pepper

1 tablespoon balsamic vinegar

2 tablespoons walnut oil

a few sprigs of watercress, pea shoots or rocket leaves (optional)

If you have a mandolin, it would be really useful. Alternatively, you just need a nice steady hand and a sharp knife. Slice the beetroot as thinly as you can. Remove the smaller slices from both ends of the beetroot, keeping only the larger rounds to serve. The smaller slices can be sprinkled with vinegar and kept in the fridge for using another day.

Lightly toast the walnuts in a dry frying pan and then roughly chop.

Mix together the ricotta, crème fraîche, chopped herbs, lemon zest and season with salt and pepper.

The thin slices of beetroot can now be arranged on plates, with a nice scoop of herbed ricotta next to them or in the middle. Sprinkle with the nuts and drizzle the balsamic vinegar and walnut oil around the outside. Finish with a few leaves on the plate to garnish and serve.

**PS . . .** The Garlic Melba Toasts (see page 181) are a great accompaniment to serve with this.

# ROASTED RED WINE MUSHROOMS WITH BLUE CHEESE AND SPINACH BAKED RISOTTO

The rich red wine marinade and all of the flavours that roast into the mushrooms are so delicious this becomes a really juicy, meaty dish.

• SERVES 6   • TAKES 20 MINUTES, PLUS 1 HOUR MARINATING AND 25 MINUTES IN THE OVEN

*for the mushrooms*

2 cloves of garlic, crushed

leaves from 2 sprigs of oregano

a handful of basil leaves

1 tablespoon tomato purée

4 tablespoons olive oil

1 tablespoon balsamic vinegar

sea salt and freshly ground black pepper

6 large portobello or field/flat mushrooms

100ml red wine

*for the risotto*

50g butter

1 onion, finely chopped

450g risotto rice

150ml white wine

1.2 litres hot vegetable stock

sea salt and freshly ground black pepper

250g blue cheese, such as Gorgonzola, Dolcelatte, Danish Blue or Stilton

150g baby spinach leaves

50g pine nuts

Whizz the garlic, oregano, basil, tomato purée, olive oil and balsamic vinegar in a mini chopper or small food processor until fairly fine. Season with salt and pepper. Rub this paste into the mushrooms, smearing it lightly into the gills. Place in a dish and pour over the red wine. Leave to marinate for 1 hour, basting a couple of times.

Preheat the oven to 200°C/fan 180°C/gas 6.

To make the risotto, melt just half of the butter in an ovenproof pan or casserole dish and gently sauté the onion until it has softened. Add the rice and stir around until it is coated in the butter before adding the white wine. Cook until half of the wine has been absorbed.

Transfer the mushrooms and wine to a roasting tray and place in the oven to roast for 25 minutes.

Add the hot stock to the rice with a twist of black pepper and a pinch of salt (not too much salt as the blue cheese will give some saltiness when added). Stir briefly and cover with a tight-fitting lid or tin foil and bake in the oven for 18 minutes, until just cooked. Remove the risotto from the oven, stir in the cheese, spinach and remaining butter and leave to sit for 5 minutes.

By now the mushrooms should be tender and starting to release their juices. When they are ready, remove from the oven.

Lightly toast the pine nuts in a dry frying pan.

Serve the risotto on warm plates and scatter over the pine nuts. Either leave the mushrooms whole or slice in half and sit on top of the risotto. Spoon any juices over them and serve straight away.

PS . . . The risotto can be partly prepared ahead of time. Once you have added the white wine and it has been absorbed by the rice, remove from the heat and then continue with the rest of the recipe 25 minutes before it is needed.

# RHUBARB MARSHMALLOW MERINGUE ROULADE

No matter how full people become, no one will be able to resist this indulgent dessert. To enjoy it at its best, make the meringue ahead of time, then roll up with the filling at the last minute (otherwise the meringue may become a little too squishy).

• SERVES 6   • TAKES 35 MINUTES, PLUS 25 MINUTES IN THE OVEN

*for the meringue*

4 large egg whites

175g caster sugar

1 teaspoon cornflour

1 teaspoon lemon juice

1 teaspoon vanilla extract

2 tablespoons sifted icing sugar, for dusting

*for the filling*

400g trimmed rhubarb

50g caster sugar

200ml double cream

½ teaspoon rose water

*You will also need a baking tray approximately 35cm x 25cm x 2cm deep*

First of all, line the baking tray with non-stick parchment paper and lightly oil.

Preheat the oven to 160°C/fan 140°C/gas 3.

To make the meringue, whisk the egg whites until they form soft peaks (using an electric whisk will make the job far easier). Add half of the caster sugar and continue to whisk for a couple of minutes.

Mix the cornflour into the remaining sugar and add to the egg whites with the lemon juice and vanilla extract. Whisk until you have a firm, glossy consistency, a bit like shaving foam. This will take a good few minutes. Spoon and spread into the prepared baking tray. Place in the oven and cook for 25 minutes.

In the meantime, cut the rhubarb into 3–4cm lengths and place in a saucepan with the sugar and 1 tablespoon water. Ccok for about 10 minutes, turning a couple of times with a metal spoon and trying not to let all of the pieces become too mushy.

Remove the cooked meringue from the oven and leave to cool in the tin for a few minutes, then carefully turn out on to a piece of baking paper heavily dusted with the icing sugar. Cool completely.

Whip the cream with the rose water until it forms soft peaks. Fold in the rhubarb and then spread over the meringue, leaving a border of about 2cm. Carefully and loosely roll the meringue lengthways into a fat cylinder shape. Transfer to a serving plate and serve.

**PS . . .** The rhubarb can be swapped for any other fruits, such as Bramley apples, plums or gooseberries, cooked in the same way as the rhubarb but adding more or less sugar depending on taste. Fresh strawberries, raspberries or blackberries (about 400g) are also really lovely, especially if you purée half of them before folding into the cream.

# SPICY

*Spicy is always a great way to go for a dinner party: everyone I know loves a curry. Monkfish is delicious for both meat and non-meat eaters and the dessert is very cleansing and exotic. This menu will definitely have your guests singing your praises.*

# Menu

*Chickpea Fritters
with Minted Yoghurt Dressing*

*\*And to drink . . .*
Red or white will work equally well here, so go for either an aromatic
New World Viognier or a dark and leafy Chilean Carmenère.

*Aromatic Monkfish Curry
with Toasted Coconut
Steamed Basmati
Garlic and Mustard Seed Green Beans*

*\*And to drink . . .*
A white wine with a touch of sweetness is the perfect
match for lightly spiced, aromatic fish dishes
and a racy Spätlese (late-harvest)
Riesling from Germany would
be fantastic with this curry.

*Lime and Mango Mousse
with Exotic Fruit Salad*

*\*And to drink . . .*
The tropical flavours in
this dessert cry out for
an equally exotic wine
such as a late-harvest
Gewürztraminer
from Alsace.

# CHICKPEA FRITTERS WITH MINTED YOGHURT DRESSING

Chickpeas are a fantastic, versatile ingredient, full of protein, and are apparently one of the earliest cultivated vegetables – 7,500-year-old remains have been found in the Middle East. To make this dish delicious, however, I suggest you use some that are not as old as that.

• SERVES 6  • 20 MINUTES

*for the dip*
150ml natural yoghurt
1 bunch of mint,
    roughly chopped
sea salt

*for the fritters*
400g tin of chickpeas, drained
1 onion, roughly chopped
1 clove of garlic
1 green chilli, roughly chopped
1 egg
75g plain flour
¼ teaspoon turmeric
¼ teaspoon cayenne pepper
½ teaspoon ground cumin
½ teaspoon ground coriander
about 1 litre sunflower
    or vegetable oil, for frying

*to serve*
4 spring onions,
    thinly sliced on an angle
a small handful of mint
    and coriander leaves
⅓ cucumber, halved
    and thinly sliced
6 small wedges of lemon

First of all, you can prepare the dressing and keep it in the fridge until needed. Blend together the yoghurt and mint in a small food processor or using a hand blender. Season with salt and keep in the fridge.

To make the fritters, place all of the ingredients apart from the oil in a food processor and blend to give you a thick batter. This can be kept in the fridge for up to a couple of hours before cooking.

Heat enough oil in a wok or large frying pan to fill about a third full.

Working in batches, place teaspoonfuls of the fritter mixture in the hot oil and fry for a couple of minutes until golden. You want to make thirty small fritters, giving five per person. Drain on kitchen paper while making the rest.

Arrange a small salad of the spring onion, mint and coriander leaves and cucumber on the side of each plate, divide the fritters among them and either spoon the dressing around or serve in small individual dipping dishes. Add a wedge of lemon and serve.

# AROMATIC MONKFISH CURRY WITH TOASTED COCONUT

This is quite a light curry, flavoured with tamarind, ginger, coriander, coconut milk and fresh tomatoes. The lovely thing about the recipe is that the curry sauce can be made well ahead of time, then gently reheated before adding the fish. Monkfish is the perfect fish to use in the curry because its firm flesh will still hold its shape once cooked. Serve with the Steamed Basmati (see page 166) and stir-fried Garlic and Mustard Seed Green Beans (see page 167) for an impressive, elegant main course.

• SERVES 6  • 20 MINUTES, PLUS 1 HOUR COOKING TIME FOR THE SAUCE

1kg monkfish tail fillet

2 tablespoons groundnut oil

2 onions, sliced

2 handfuls of coconut flakes

1 tablespoon coriander seeds

1 teaspoon fenugreek seeds

3 cloves of garlic

4cm piece of fresh ginger, peeled and roughly chopped

1 long red chilli, seeds kept in

5 decent-sized ripe, juicy tomatoes, roughly chopped

1 tablespoon tamarind paste

10–12 curry leaves

1 tablespoon palm sugar or soft light brown sugar

1 tablespoon fish sauce

400ml tin of coconut milk

a small bunch of coriander, roughly chopped

Cut the monkfish fillets into roughly 3cm pieces and keep in the fridge until needed.

Heat the oil in a large saucepan and slowly cook the onion for about 10 minutes until it is completely softened and just starting to become golden.

Lightly toast the coconut flakes in a hot frying pan until they are just golden. Remove from the pan and keep to one side.

Add the coriander and fenugreek seeds to the frying pan and shake around until they become fragrant. Tip into a food processor, add the garlic, ginger and chilli and blend until finely chopped. Add the tomatoes and blend to a pulp. Pour into the saucepan with the onion. Add the tamarind, curry leaves, sugar and fish sauce and bring to a simmer, cooking for 5 minutes while stirring frequently.

Stir in the coconut milk, then simmer for 45 minutes, stirring occasionally, until thickened. It can now be left and reheated gently when needed.

Stir the monkfish into the sauce, return to a simmer and cook for 10 minutes. It won't take long for the monkfish to cook through. Stir in the coriander.

Use a slotted spoon to transfer the monkfish to six plates or bowls and then spoon over the sauce. Finally, scatter over the toasted coconut and serve with the basmati and green beans.

PS . . . If the cost of monkfish is a little too steep, you could replace a third to half of the quantity with large raw tiger prawns.

# STEAMED BASMATI

Follow this method and you should have perfect, fluffy rice every time. The rice is cooked in a measured amount of water so that by the time all the liquid has been absorbed it will be ready, meaning there is no draining of gloopy, starchy water required. The spices are optional but do give a great flavour to complement any curry.

• SERVES 6   • 15 MINUTES

500g basmati rice
700ml cold water
a pinch of salt
6 whole cloves
6 cardamom pods,
   lightly crushed with
   the back of a spoon

Wash the rice in plenty of cold water by shaking it in a sieve under a running tap for a few minutes. This will get rid of any excess starch, which can make the rice stodgy.

Put the rice in a medium to large saucepan. Add the water, salt and the spices. Place over a medium heat, bring to the boil and cover immediately with a tight-fitting lid. Turn the heat to low and leave to cook for 10 minutes without lifting the lid at all.

After 10 minutes, turn off the heat but keep the lid firmly in place because the rice will carry on cooking. Leave for 5 minutes before removing the lid (though it will stay hot for up to 20 minutes if you leave the lid on).

Fluff up the rice with a fork. All of the water should be completely absorbed and your rice should be wonderfully light and fluffy. Serve with your curry, either with the spices left in or lifted out beforehand.

# GARLIC AND MUSTARD SEED GREEN BEANS

This tasty little side dish not only adds colour, but also a lovely flavour to accompany the curry. I guarantee these greens won't be left on the side of anyone's plate.

• SERVES 6   • 10 MINUTES

400g fine green beans, trimmed

3 tablespoons groundnut oil

1 teaspoon brown
   mustard seeds

2 cloves of garlic,
   thinly sliced

1 onion, finely chopped

sea salt

Blanch the beans in boiling salted water until they are just beginning to become tender. This can be done ahead of time and the beans then kept cool.

Heat the oil in a wok or large frying pan. Add the mustard seeds and fry for about 30 seconds until they start to pop in the pan.

Add the garlic and onion and cook until the onions are softened and starting to become golden.

Add the green beans and stir-fry over a high heat for a few minutes until they are heated through and coated with the onion, garlic and mustard seeds. Season with salt and serve with the curry and rice.

# LIME AND MANGO MOUSSE WITH EXOTIC FRUIT SALAD

After a spicy starter and main course, you'll be ready for a super-light, refreshing dessert.

• SERVES 6   • 30 MINUTES, PLUS OVERNIGHT SETTING

*for the mousse*

3 leaves of gelatine

1 ripe mango, peeled

finely grated zest of 2 limes and juice of 4 limes (about 100ml)

175g caster sugar

2 egg whites

200ml natural yoghurt

*for the fruit salad*

a small selection of fresh ripe fruit, such as pineapple, kiwi, mango, lychee, papaya, passion fruit, guava, etc.

To make the mousse, soak the gelatine leaves in cold water for 5 minutes to soften.

Chop the mango flesh and blend to a really smooth purée.

Place the lime juice and zest in small saucepan with half of the sugar. Stir over a low heat until the sugar dissolves. Squeeze the water out of the gelatine and stir into the pan until it has dissolved. Leave to cool.

Pour the lime and gelatine mixture into a jug and add enough of the mango purée to reach 250ml. Any remaining mango can be kept to one side.

In a large bowl, whisk the egg whites until they form soft peaks. Gradually whisk in the remaining caster sugar and keep whisking until the meringue is firm and glossy.

Mix the lime and mango mixture with the yoghurt and the fold this into the meringue.

Spoon into glasses and keep in the fridge overnight to set.

Prepare your chosen fruit, cut into small pieces and mix together. If there is any mango purée left over, this can be added.

To serve, place the mousses on plates and spoon the fruit on top.

**PS . . .** Those who might be at risk from the effects of salmonella food poisoning (the elderly, pregnant women, young children and those suffering from immune deficiency diseases) should consult their GP with any concerns about eating raw eggs.

# READY, STEADY, DINNER PARTY

*I mentioned in the introduction to this chapter that organizing a dinner party seems like a great idea at the time but, as the date gets closer, can make you panic. This section is for when you've just had one of those weeks or perhaps have even forgotten that you're having a dinner party. These are recipes that mostly use ready-prepared ingredients (basically short cuts) and it certainly doesn't get any simpler than stirring a bought dressed crab into home-made mashed potato. It'll seem as if Gary Rhodes himself is in the kitchen helping you cook.*

# Menu

*Sweet Onion and Dolcelatte Tarts
  with Pear and Walnut Salad*

*∗And to drink . . .*

  A soft, cherry-scented Valpolicella from northern
  Italy has exactly the acidity needed to cut through
  the sweetness of the onions and the richness of
  the pastry and blue cheese.

*Roast Cod
  with Dressed Crab Mash and Lobster Sauce*

*∗And to drink . . .*

  The rich shellfish flavours in this luxurious
  dish deserve a very stylish oaked Chardonnay
  such as a Meursault or a Chassagne-Montrachet
  from Burgundy's Côte d'Or.

*Caramelized Crêpes
  with Bitter Orange and Brandy Sauce*

*∗And to drink . . .*

  Try the honeyed, citric flavours of an Australian
  botrytized Semillon with this twist on a seventies classic.

# SWEET ONION AND DOLCELATTE TARTS WITH PEAR AND WALNUT SALAD

Ready, steady, go . . . a super-speedy starter that doesn't compromise on flavour.

• SERVES 6  • 25 MINUTES

375g ready-rolled
  puff pastry

olive oil, for brushing

6 tablespoons caramelized
  onions, from a jar

1 tablespoon thyme leaves

250g Dolcelatte cheese,
  diced or broken into
  small pieces

2 small ripe pears,
  cored and cut into
  small pieces

100g watercress

2 sticks of celery,
  thinly sliced

a small handful of
  walnut halves

2 tablespoons walnut oil

2 teaspoons balsamic vinegar

sea salt and freshly
  ground black pepper

Preheat the oven to 200°C/fan 180°C/gas 6.

Cut the pastry into six circles about 10cm in diameter using a large pastry cutter or by cutting around a small plate. Place on a lightly greased or non-stick baking tray and score a small border of about 5mm to 1cm around the inside edge of each one. Brush the border with olive oil.

Spread the caramelized onions on top of each piece of puff pastry, within the border. Scatter over the thyme leaves and half of the cheese. Place in the oven for 12 to 15 minutes until the pastry is golden.

While the pastry is cooking, toss together the pears, watercress, celery, walnuts, walnut oil and balsamic vinegar. Season with salt and pepper and arrange on six plates.

Remove the tarts from the oven and top with the remaining cheese. Return to the oven for a few minutes for the cheese to just start melting and then serve with the salad.

# ROAST COD WITH DRESSED CRAB MASH AND LOBSTER SAUCE

To make life less manic, prepare the mash and sauce as early as you can and set aside to finish off at the last minute. That leaves the cod. Well, all you need to do is put it in the oven – simple. If you fancy a vegetable to serve with this, some wilted spinach or tenderstem broccoli would go really well.

• SERVES 6   • 40 MINUTES

*for the mash*

1.5kg floury potatoes, such as Maris Piper or King Edward

50g butter

100ml single cream

1 dressed crab

a squeeze of lemon juice

sea salt and black pepper

*for the sauce*

1 tablespoon olive oil

1 onion, finely chopped

1 red chilli, deseeded and finely chopped

415g tin of lobster bisque

a good splash of brandy

1 tablespoon tomato purée

4 tomatoes, quartered, deseeded and diced

2 tablespoons single cream

2 tablespoons finely chopped chives

sea salt and black pepper

*for the cod*

½ lemon

6 x 150–200g thick cod fillets, skin on

olive oil

sea salt and black pepper

Preheat the oven to 200°C/fan 180°C/gas 6.

Peel the potatoes, cut into large, equal-sized chunks and rinse under the tap. Cook in boiling salted water until tender. Drain well and mash with the butter and a couple of tablespoons of the cream until smooth. This can now be covered with clingfilm and kept aside until you are ready to finish it off.

To make the lobster sauce, heat the olive oil in a frying pan and gently sauté the onion and chilli until the onion is softened. Pour in the lobster bisque, brandy and tomato purée. Bring to a simmer and cook for 5 to 8 minutes, or until it has reduced in quantity by about half. You can leave the sauce at this stage to finish when needed.

Squeeze some lemon juice over the cod, rub with olive oil and season well with salt and pepper. Place on a baking tray, skin-side down, and roast for 15 minutes until the flesh is just opaque.

Return the mash to the heat and, once it is hot, stir in the dressed crab meat and remaining cream. Add a squeeze of lemon juice and season with salt and pepper if needed.

Stir the diced tomatoes and single cream into the lobster sauce, gently cooking until they have heated through. Add the chopped chives and season with salt and pepper.

Spoon the dressed crab mash on to warm plates, sit the cod on top and spoon over the lobster sauce.

# CARAMELIZED CRÊPES WITH BITTER ORANGE AND BRANDY SAUCE

These are deliciously sweet and quite filling, so you might find serving just one crêpe per person is enough. If that is the case, cut down all of the ingredients by half. I must say, however, I can manage two quite easily!

• SERVES 6   • 25 MINUTES

200g caster sugar

8 tablespoons fine-cut marmalade

12 ready-made pancakes/crêpes

50g butter, melted

3 tablespoons brandy

2 tablespoons fresh orange juice

extra-thick cream or ice-cream, to serve

Place the caster sugar on a flat plate.

Spread a layer of marmalade over each pancake/crêpe and then fold in half and in half again to give you twelve triangles (you will have some marmalade left over). The pancakes can be kept in the fridge at this stage until needed.

Brush both sides of the pancakes lightly with the melted butter and then press into the caster sugar, coating fairly generously.

Heat a large non-stick pancake or frying pan over a high heat and brush with a little of the melted butter. Cooking a few at a time, fry the folded pancakes/crêpes for about 1 minute on each side until the sugar has caramelized. Keep the crêpes warm.

Add the remaining butter and marmalade to the pan and, once it is bubbling, pour in the brandy, allowing it to flambé using the gas flame or a lit match if you have an electric hob. Stir in the orange juice and then pour around the outside of the caramelized crêpes.

Serve two crêpes per person with a dollop of extra-thick cream or a scoop of ice-cream.

# PREPARE AHEAD

*When you know you'll be running round like a headless chicken on the day of your dinner party (meeting your mates for a coffee, buying a new outfit, tidying your house, practising your cocktails . . . those sorts of things), this menu is a must. You can prepare the lion's share of the food up to two days before the actual party, leaving only last-minute finishing to do that evening, easy peasy.*

# Menu

*Leek and White Bean Soup*
*with Sage Butter and Garlic Melba Toasts*

*\*And to drink . . .*
The gentle flavours and creamy texture
of this soup need a subtle, refreshing,
food-friendly white such as a Soave
or Grüner Veltliner.

*Redcurrant Venison Bourguignon*
*with Spring Onion Potato Cakes*

*\*And to drink . . .*
With a rich, gamey dish such as this, only the
best will do and a plum- and truffle-scented
aged Pinot Noir from Burgundy will taste sublime.
Premier or Grand Cru if you can afford it . . .

*Molten Chocolate Orange Puddings*

*\*And to drink . . .*
Chocolate is notoriously difficult to match,
but in this case a lusciously sweet Tokaji
from Hungary will pick up on the orange
flavour in the pudding as well as having
enough acidity to cut through the richness
of the chocolate.

# LEEK AND WHITE BEAN SOUP WITH SAGE BUTTER AND GARLIC MELBA TOASTS

This is a great starter because both the soup and Melba toasts can be made in advance, making it really simple and stress-free. All you need to do is make the sage butter at the last minute, which takes no time at all. These aren't huge portions of soup, which is best when serving it as a starter, especially before the rich Redcurrant Venison Bourguignon.

• SERVES 6   • 45 MINUTES

*for the soup*

25g butter
2 medium leeks, chopped
1 stick of celery, chopped
1 bay leaf
2 x 400g tins of butter beans, drained
900ml chicken or vegetable stock
300ml milk
sea salt and freshly ground black pepper

*for the garlic Melba toasts*

3 pieces of medium-sliced white bread
2 tablespoons garlic-infused oil

*for the sage butter*

50g butter
about 6 large sage leaves, finely chopped
2 tablespoons lemon juice

To prepare the soup, melt the butter in a saucepan and, once it is bubbling, add the leeks, celery and bay leaf. Cook without colouring for about 10 minutes before adding the butter beans and stock. Bring to a simmer and cook for 15 minutes.

Add the milk to the soup, season with salt and pepper and return to a simmer before removing from the heat. Fish out the bay leaf and leave the soup to cool for a while before liquidizing until smooth. If you blend it too soon, the piping-hot steam can blow the top off your liquidizer – a lesson I have learned the hard way!

To make the soup silky smooth, pass through a sieve into a saucepan. When you are ready for the soup, gently heat through.

To make the toast, preheat the grill to a medium heat. Remove the crusts from the bread, brush the bread with the garlic oil and lightly toast on both sides. Cut through each slice horizontally, so you end up with six very thin pieces. Scrape any soft bread from the surface and cut each piece in half diagonally, giving you twelve triangles. Brush the untoasted sides lightly with the oil and return the bread to the grill for up to 1 minute until each piece is curled up at the edges and has become nice and crunchy.

Pour the hot soup into bowls and finally make the sage butter. Melt the butter in a hot frying pan and, once it is foaming, throw in the sage and fry for a few seconds. Remove the pan from the heat and add the lemon juice, then spoon a little around each bowl of soup. Serve straight away with the Garlic Melba Toast on the side.

# REDCURRANT VENISON BOURGUIGNON WITH SPRING ONION POTATO CAKES

Wonderfully rich and full of different flavours, yet so simple to prepare. If you can't get hold of any venison, braising steak can be used, but do try venison, even frozen, because it has a lovely flavour and is exceptionally lean.

• SERVES 6   • 25 MINUTES, PLUS 2½ HOURS COOKING AND 30 MINUTES FOR POTATO CAKES

500ml Burgundy wine

4 tablespoons redcurrant jelly

2 tablespoons olive oil

200g diced pancetta
  or lardons

18 baby onions
  or shallots, peeled

sea salt and freshly
  ground black pepper

1.5–2kg diced venison

50g plain flour

3 sticks of celery,
  sliced into 1cm pieces

4 cloves of garlic, crushed

1 bay leaf, sprig of thyme
  and 2 peeled strips of
  orange zest, tied with a
  piece of string

1 tablespoon
  Worcestershire sauce

300ml beef stock

25g butter

200g button mushrooms

2 tablespoons chopped parsley

In a small saucepan, heat the wine with the redcurrant jelly until the jelly dissolves.

Meanwhile, heat 1 tablespoon of the olive oil in a large ovenproof casserole dish and brown the pancetta or lardons. Remove with a slotted spoon and add the onions or shallots. Cook over a medium to high heat, stirring until golden.

Season the venison and toss in the flour (easily done in a large sandwich bag). Add to the pan along with the pancetta or lardons, the celery, garlic, bay leaf, thyme and orange zest, Worcestershire sauce, beef stock, salt, pepper and the red wine and redcurrant jelly mixture. Stir and gently bring to a simmer. Cover and cook for 2 hours, stirring occasionally.

This can be made a day or two in advance, left to cool and kept in the fridge. About 1 hour before eating, the bourguignon can be gently returned to a simmer.

Cook the potatoes until tender. Drain and mash until smooth.

Gently fry the spring onions in 25g butter for a minute or so until softened but not coloured. Stir into the mashed potato along with a good grating of nutmeg and the flour and season.

Shape into small or large cakes and place on a flat plate or tray lined with greaseproof paper. Cover with greaseproof paper and refrigerate until needed.

Preheat the oven to 160°C/fan 140°C/gas 3.

Melt 25g butter. Once bubbling, add the mushrooms and toss around until golden. Add to the casserole dish and simmer gently or cook in the oven for about 30 to 40 minutes.

*for the potato cakes*

1kg floury potatoes, peeled and cut into chunks

2 bunches of spring onions, sliced

50g butter

freshly grated nutmeg

3 tablespoons flour

sea salt and freshly ground black pepper

1 tablespoon olive oil

Melt 25g butter in a large frying pan with the olive oil. When the butter is bubbling, fry the potato cakes for a few minutes on each side until golden. You may need to do this in batches. Place on a baking tray and put in the oven to completely heat through for about 10 minutes.

Take out the herb bundle and scatter with parsley before serving the bourguignon with the potato cakes and vegetables of your choice.

# MOLTEN CHOCOLATE ORANGE PUDDINGS

These are just like posh Jaffa Cakes. I shouldn't need to say any more to tempt you into making them, apart from the fact that they are surprisingly easy to prepare.

• SERVES 6  • 30 MINUTES, PLUS 10 MINUTES COOKING

*for the syrup*
2 large oranges
150g caster sugar

*for the puddings*
115g plain chocolate, chopped
115g unsalted butter
3 whole eggs
2 egg yolks
50g caster sugar
finely grated zest of 1 orange
50g plain flour

*for the orange cream*
150ml double cream
1–2 tablespoons Cointreau
 or Grand Marnier
1 tablespoon caster sugar

*to serve*
dark chocolate,
 to grate or shave over
cocoa powder, to dust

*You will also need
 six x 150–200ml ramekin
 dishes, buttered*

To make the syrup, use a zester to peel strips of orange zest from one of the oranges. Place in a small saucepan with the juice from both oranges and the caster sugar. Stir over a low heat for a couple of minutes until the sugar dissolves. Increase the heat and boil for about 5 minutes until the liquid thickens slightly. Leave to cool and keep at room temperature, not in the fridge, until needed.

Preheat the oven to 190°C/fan 170°C/gas 5.

To make the chocolate orange puddings, melt the chocolate and butter in a bowl over a pan of simmering water or, alternatively, gently melt in the microwave. Leave to cool slightly.

Whisk the eggs, egg yolks, sugar and orange zest with an electric hand whisk until they have doubled in volume. Be patient, it will take a good few minutes. Sift the flour on top and fold in, along with the melted chocolate butter. Spoon into the buttered ramekins and either cook for 10 minutes to serve straight away or you can keep them covered in the fridge for a couple of days and cook them when required (make sure you return them to room temperature before cooking or just keep at room temperature for up to 1 hour).

For the orange cream, whisk the cream until it starts to thicken. Add the Cointreau or Grand Marnier and caster sugar and continue to whisk until it reaches a soft peak.

To serve the Chocolate Orange Puddings, turn them out on to plates, grate or shave (using a vegetable peeler) a little chocolate over the top of each one and dust with cocoa. Spoon the orange syrup around the outside, place a spoonful of orange cream next to the sponges and serve straight away.

# FINE DINING

*Two menus, split by seasons, using the best ingredients and served with fine wine. These recipes are for special occasions only – birthdays, anniversaries, a new season of* The X Factor . . .

*First, my spring/summer menu, packed with fresh seasonal ingredients.*

# Menu One

*Pan-Fried Mackerel*
*with Pea Shoots and Summer Potato Salad*

*\*And to drink . . .*

Depending on your mood, try either a fruity southern French rosé
or a peach- and herb-scented Albariño from north-west Spain.

*Artichoke and Truffle-crusted Rack of Lamb*
*with Creamy White Beans*

*\*And to drink . . .*

The subtle yet meaty, pepper and spiced blackberry flavours of a northern
Rhône syrah would be the perfect match for this heady lamb dish.

*Muscat and Vanilla Poached Peaches*
*with Clotted Cream*

*\*And to drink . . .*

Stick to the Muscat theme with this dessert and go for
an aromatic and floral Muscat de Beaumes-de-Venise.

# PAN-FRIED MACKEREL WITH PEA SHOOTS AND SUMMER POTATO SALAD

This is a lovely light starter that will work just as well with watercress instead of the pea shoots and is equally delicious with pan-fried or smoked salmon and trout instead of the mackerel. Prepare the salad ahead, leaving you just the fish to fry at the last minute.

• SERVES 6   • TAKES 30–40 MINUTES

400g waxy new potatoes, such as Charlotte

100g fine green beans

250g asparagus tips

100g peas (fresh or frozen)

2 small shallots, finely chopped

2½ tablespoons hot horseradish sauce

125ml crème fraîche

a small bunch of mint, chopped

a squeeze of lemon juice

sea salt and freshly ground black pepper

1 tablespoon olive oil

6 small mackerel fillets

50g pea shoots

Boil the potatoes in salted water until they are tender. Drain, leave to cool and then cut into quarter wedges.

In a separate saucepan, blanch the green beans and asparagus for just a couple of minutes and then refresh in iced water to stop them cooking further. If you are using frozen peas, they just need to be defrosted. If you're using fresh ones, then these can be boiled in salted water until tender. They should take about 5 to 8 minutes. Also refresh in cold water.

Mix together the shallots, horseradish, crème fraîche, chopped mint and lemon juice and season with salt and pepper. Carefully mix in the potatoes, green beans, asparagus and peas.

To cook the mackerel, heat a large frying pan and add the oil. Season the mackerel fillets on both sides with a little salt and pepper. Place in the pan and cook, skin-side down, for 2 to 3 minutes until the skin is crisp and golden (press on the fillets lightly if they start to curl upwards to get a crisp effect all over). Turn each fillet over and cook for a further minute. If your pan isn't big enough to do all the fillets at the same time, just keep the cooked ones warm on a plate.

Serve the mackerel, skin-side up, next to a nice bundle of pea shoots topped with a spoonful of the potato salad. Finally, scatter over some more pea shoots.

# ARTICHOKE AND TRUFFLE-CRUSTED RACK OF LAMB WITH CREAMY WHITE BEANS

To make your main course as stress-free as possible, coat the lamb in the artichoke and truffle crust in advance, keep in the fridge and return to room temperature just before roasting. Also delicious with baby courgettes sautéed in olive oil with lemon juice and zest.

• SERVES 6 • 45 MINUTES

50g ciabatta bread

1 tablespoon chopped oregano leaves

30g black summer truffles, either fresh or preserved in a jar

75g walnut pieces

50g Parmesan cheese, finely grated

olive oil

sea salt and freshly ground black pepper

3 racks of lamb (6–8 bones per rack), French-trimmed

3 tablespoons artichoke paste (see PS . . . )

*for the beans*

2 tablespoons olive oil

3 shallots, finely chopped

2 x 400g tins of cannellini beans, drained

150ml white wine

200ml chicken stock

sea salt and freshly ground black pepper

150ml low-fat crème fraîche

Preheat the oven to 220°C/fan 200°C/gas 8.

Place the bread and oregano leaves in a food processor and blitz to crumbs. Add the truffles and the walnut pieces and pulse to a coarse crumb consistency. Stir in the Parmesan and 3 tablespoons of olive oil and season.

Season the lamb all over with salt and pepper. Heat a trickle of olive oil in a roasting tray or large ovenproof frying pan over a medium heat. Add the lamb, fat-side down, and fry for 5 to 8 minutes until the fat is melting and becoming golden. Increase the heat and brown all over to seal the meat. Remove the lamb and place on a board.

Spread the artichoke paste over the fat side of the racks of lamb and then press the crust on top.

Return the lamb, crust-side up, to the roasting tray or frying pan. Roast for 20 minutes for a pinkish finish (longer if you prefer your lamb well done).

Meanwhile, in a wide saucepan, heat the oil and sauté the shallots until softened but not coloured. Add the beans, wine and stock. Bring to a simmer and cook gently for about 10 minutes. Season and lightly mash, breaking down some of the beans. Stir in the crème fraîche and heat through.

Remove the lamb from the oven and leave to rest for about 5 minutes. Carve the rested lamb by slicing each rack in half, giving three to four bones per portion.

PS . . . If you can't find ready-made artichoke paste, blend a jar of marinated artichokes antipasti with a little of the oil to a paste, or purée some tinned ones with olive oil.

# MUSCAT AND VANILLA POACHED PEACHES WITH CLOTTED CREAM

This deliciously fresh and simple dessert is perfect for entertaining because the peaches are best made the day before serving and kept in the fridge overnight.

• SERVES 6   • 20 MINUTES, PLUS OVERNIGHT CHILLING

400ml Muscat dessert wine
250g caster sugar
1 vanilla pod, split
1 large orange, zested with a potato peeler
6 ripe peaches
200g clotted cream
6 mint sprigs to garnish
18 raspberries

Pour the Muscat nto a saucepan just big enough to fit in the peaches. Add the sugar, vanilla pod and strips of orange zest. Place over a medium heat and gently bring to a simmer until the sugar has dissolved. Add the peaches and return to a gentle simmer.

Poach the peaches for about 8 to 10 minutes until they feel tender when pierced with a sharp knife. If they're not totally immersed in the liquid, carefully turn halfway through.

Remove the peaches from the pan and, as soon as they are cool enough to handle, remove the skin. It should peel away really easily. Return the peaches to the poaching liquid and chill for at least 2 hours, but overnight would be preferable.

An hour or so before you plan to serve the peaches, pour half of the poaching liquid into a small saucepan and bring to the boil. Reduce in quantity by about half or until it is looking syrupy. Remove from the heat, cool and then chill.

Serve the peaches on plates next to a scroll of clotted cream (done by scooping the cream with a warm dessert spoon), a sprig of mint and three raspberries each. Finish by spooning over some of the syrup and serve straight away.

# FINE DINING

*My autumn/winter menu allows you to showcase fresh British scallops in the starter, followed by a traditional fillet of beef dish and coffee panna cottas.*

# Menu Two

*Seared Scallops*
  *with Smoky Leeks and Orange Butter*

*\*And to drink . . .*

The rustic power of a smoky Roussillon white is exactly what's needed to match the flavours in this wintery scallop dish.

*Fillet of Beef*
  *with Madeira Sauce*

    *Celeriac and Chanterelle Dauphinois*

*\*And to drink . . .*

A good Bordeaux red is the obvious choice here, but given the sauce you could be adventurous and try one of the drier styles of Madeira such as a Sercial or Verdelho.

*Cappuccino Panna Cotta*
  *with Hazelnut Syrup*

*\*And to drink . . .*

When it's good, Italian Vin Santo has the most wonderful toasted nut and sultana flavours that would be the perfect compliment to this creamy, coffee-scented panna cotta.

# SEARED SCALLOPS
# WITH SMOKY LEEKS AND ORANGE BUTTER

This is such a stylish-looking starter and tastes divine. The method may look fiddly, but it really is very quick and easy to make, provided you get everything prepared before you start cooking. The sauce can be made ahead of time and warmed very gently just before it's needed.

• SERVES 6  • 20 MINUTES

juice of 1 large orange

125ml chicken or fish stock

200g chilled butter,
  cut into cubes, plus an
  extra knob for the scallops

sea salt and freshly ground
  black pepper

olive oil

6 slices of smoked streaky
  bacon, cut into fine strips

1 large leek, very thinly sliced

18 large scallops,
  with or without the roe
  attached (it's up to you)

First of all, to make the sauce, bring the orange juice to the boil in a small saucepan and reduce in quantity by a third. Add the stock, bring to the boil and then whisk in the butter, a little at a time, until it thickens the sauce slightly. Season with salt and pepper and keep warm to one side.

Heat a frying pan or wok with a drop of olive oil and cook the bacon pieces until they are golden and crispy. Remove from the pan and drain on kitchen paper.

Add the leek to the frying pan or wok and cook over a high heat until just tender, tossing it around in the pan and adding a splash of water if necessary to prevent it from burning on the edges. Return half of the bacon to the pan or wok and toss into the leek. The remaining bacon is to be used at the end.

To cook the scallops, heat a drizzle of oil in a large frying pan. Once it is hot, add the scallops with a small knob of butter. Cook for 1 to 2 minutes until golden with dark tinges on the edges, then turn them over and cook for a further 1 to 2 minutes. Remove from the pan and season with salt.

To serve, place three individual spoonfuls of smoky leeks on each plate and sit a scallop on top of each pile of leeks. Scatter a few bacon pieces over the leeks and finally spoon around the orange butter sauce. Serve straight away.

# FILLET OF BEEF WITH MADEIRA SAUCE

This is a rather luxurious treat. When serving a fabulous piece of meat like beef fillet, your best bet is to cook it simply like this.

• SERVES 6   • 20 MINUTES, PLUS 20–50 MINUTES COOKING

1kg fillet of beef

sea salt and freshly ground black pepper

2 tablespoons olive oil

2 red onions, thickly sliced

a small bunch of thyme

150ml Madeira

500ml beef stock (fresh if possible) or the mushroom soaking liquid from the Celeriac and Chanterelle Dauphinois (see opposite) topped up to 500ml with beef stock

1 teaspoon Dijon mustard

Preheat the oven to 200°C/fan 180°C/gas 6.

Season the beef with salt and plenty of black pepper. Heat the oil in a sturdy roasting tray on the hob and, when it's very hot, quickly sear the beef fillet until it's evenly browned all over.

Remove from the heat and scatter the onions and thyme around the fillet. Cook in the oven for 20 to 25 minutes for rare, 40 minutes for medium or 50 minutes for well-done beef. Halfway through the cooking time, turn the onions in the tray and pour over the Madeira.

Once the beef is cooked, remove from the tray and keep warm while it rests for a good 10 minutes.

Place the tray over a medium heat and add the beef stock. Boil until it has reduced by half. Stir in the Dijon mustard and season to taste. Stain through a sieve to remove the onions and thyme. The sauce will be fairly loose, working really well with the rich Celeriac and Chanterelle Dauphinois (see opposite). If you prefer to serve a creamy sauce, a good glug of double cream can be added at this stage.

Slice the beef as thickly or thinly as you wish and serve with the sauce, the Celeriac and Chanterelle Dauphinois and a green veg such as buttered spinach, green beans or tenderstem broccoli.

# CELERIAC AND CHANTERELLE DAUPHINOIS

A rich, flavoursome accompaniment to the beef, this can be made in one large dish or, for a stylish touch, you could bake in smaller receptacles (one for each guest).

• SERVES 6    • 35 MINUTES, PLUS ABOUT 1 HOUR 10 MINUTES IN THE OVEN

50g dried chanterelle
mushrooms

600g celeriac

500g white potatoes
(Desiree or Cara
are a good choice)

3 cloves of garlic,
thinly sliced

375ml single cream

sea salt and freshly ground
black pepper

25g butter

*You will also need a buttered
2-litre ovenproof dish or
six individual dishes, each
about 300ml in capacity*

Preheat the oven to 180°C/fan 160°C/gas 4.

Cover the chanterelle mushrooms with 250ml hot water and leave to soak for about 30 minutes.

Peel the celeriac and potatoes and slice them really thinly. If you have a mandolin or a slicing attachment on your food processor, then use it because it will make life easier. Place in a bowl with the garlic,cream and salt and pepper and lightly mix everything together.

Drain the chanterelles, straining and reserving the liquid, if using for the Fillet of Beef with Madeira Sauce (see opposite), and lightly squeeze any excess liquid out of the mushrooms.

Layer up the celeriac and potatoes, scattering the mushrooms among the layers as you go. Finish with a neat layer of celeriac and potatoes, then add any cream left behind in the bowl. Dot the top with a little butter and place on a baking tray. Cover loosely with foil.

Cook for 30 minutes and then remove the foil. Continue to cook for a further 30 to 40 minutes until the celeriac and potatoes are tender and golden on top. If you are making individual ones, they will need less cooking time (about 15 minutes will be fine). To check they are done, pierce with a skewer and if they still seem hard, bake for a further 10 minutes or until they are done. Remove from the oven and leave for 10 minutes before serving.

**PS . . .** If you are making this when fresh chanterelle mushrooms are available, then 150g will be plenty.

# CAPPUCCINO PANNA COTTA WITH HAZELNUT SYRUP

Something to perk you up ready for the after-dinner games.

• SERVES 6   • 20 MINUTES, PLUS AT LEAST 2 HOURS SETTING TIME

*for the panna cotta*

3 leaves gelatine

450ml single cream

100g icing sugar

3 teaspoons instant coffee granules

1 teaspoon vanilla extract

300ml natural-set yoghurt

a small block of dark chocolate, for shaving

*for the syrup*

75g caster sugar

3 tablespoons Frangelico liqueur

3 tablespoons chopped roasted hazelnuts

*You will also need six 150ml moulds, such as plastic or metal pudding moulds, teacups or ramekins, lightly greased with vegetable oil (the easiest to use are the plastic basins)*

Soak the gelatine leaves in cold water for 5 minutes.

Place the cream in a saucepan over a medium heat and stir in the sugar, coffee granules and vanilla extract until the coffee has completely dissolved. Gently bring to the boil, stirring occasionally. Remove from the heat and stir in the gelatine until it has dissolved (squeeze out the excess water first). Leave to cool for 5 minutes before stirring in the yoghurt until smooth, using a whisk if necessary.

Pour into the greased moulds and set in the fridge for about 2 hours or overnight if you can.

To make the hazelnut syrup, place the caster sugar, Frangelico and 50ml water into a saucepan over a medium heat. Stir until the sugar has dissolved and bring to the boil. Leave to boil for about 3 minutes until slightly syrupy, then cool.

Turn the set panna cottas out on to plates. If they won't come out very easily, slide a sharp knife down the side to break the air seal or very briefly dip the moulds into hot water.

Stir the hazelnuts into the syrup and then spoon over the top of the panna cottas. Finish by scattering them with shavings of chocolate.

**PS . . .** As an alternative to Frangelico, you could use the almond-flavoured liqueur Amaretto. A couple of biscotti or cantucci biscuits would also be nice served on the side of the plate.

# PIMP UP YOUR DINNER PARTY

*These recipes will add that little something extra to your dinner party, with four additional courses to wow your guests. Get their taste buds going with an amuse-bouche; cleanse their palates with a sorbet; give them a cheese course with some home-made biscuits; and finish with some hand-made petits fours and coffee. You might want to tell your guests to skip lunch that day.*

# Menu

## Amuse-bouches

Pea and Mint Shots
with Parma Ham Crisps
and Parmesan Straws

Scallop and Avocado Tortillas

Duck Pâté on Brioche
with Honey Pears

Rarebit Toasts
with Tomato and Chive Salad

## Sorbets/Palate Cleansers

Cucumber and Mint Sorbet

Lemon, Lime and Vodka Sorbet

Watermelon Sorbet

## Cheese Course

Apple and Pear Crisps

Fig and Apricot Chutney

Parmesan Oatcakes

Walnut and Blue
Cheese Biscuits

## Petits Fours

Chocolate Crunch Bites

Chocolate and
Hazelnut Macaroons

Peppermint Creams

# AMUSE-BOUCHES

*These give your dinner party maximum impact with minimum fuss. They are also great served as a canapé.*

## PEA AND MINT SHOTS WITH PARMA HAM CRISPS AND PARMESAN STRAWS

These can all be made ahead of time, so all you need to do is heat the soup through and garnish before serving.

• **6 SHOTS AND TWO EXTRA FULL-SIZE PORTIONS OF SOUP TO FREEZE** • **30 MINUTES**

### for the soup
1 tablespoon olive oil

1 onion, chopped

600ml chicken or vegetable stock

400g frozen peas

4 tablespoons single or double cream

2 tablespoons chopped mint leaves, plus 6 very small sprigs of mint, to garnish

sea salt and freshly ground black pepper

### for the Parmesan straws
about 100g ready-rolled puff pastry

1 egg yolk

1 tablespoon finely grated Parmesan cheese

### for the Parma ham crisps
2 tablespoons olive oil

2 slices of Parma ham

Preheat the oven to 220°C/fan 200°C/gas 8.

To make the soup, heat the oil in a saucepan and sauté the onion for about 5 minutes until it's softened but not coloured. Add the stock and, as soon as it is boiling, the peas. Return to the boil and cook for 3 minutes. Stir in the cream and mint and season with salt and pepper.

Blitz the soup in a food processor or blender until smooth. About two-thirds of the soup can be kept in the fridge or freezer and used another time for a lunch or a starter. The remaining third is to use for this recipe.

To make the Parmesan straws, cut the pastry into thin strips and place on a greased baking tray. Brush with the egg yolk and scatter over the Parmesan. Bake in the oven for about 10 minutes until golden and crispy.

To make the Parma ham crisps, heat the olive oil in a small frying pan. Tear or cut each piece of ham into three and, once the oil is hot, fry for just a few seconds until golden and crispy. Drain on kitchen paper.

Just before serving, heat the soup until hot but not boiling. Pour into six large shot glasses or espresso cups. Garnish each one with a small mint sprig. Sit on a plate and place the Parma ham crisps and Parmesan straws by the side and serve.

# SCALLOP AND AVOCADO TORTILLAS

• MAKES 6   • 15 MINUTES

1–2 flour tortillas

2 tablespoons olive oil

1 small ripe avocado

1 spring onion,
    finely chopped

juice of ½ lime,
    plus 6 slim wedges to serve

1 tablespoon
    chopped coriander

2 pinches of cayenne pepper

sea salt and freshly ground
    black pepper

6 large scallops

Cut twelve circles from the tortillas using a 4 to 5cm pastry cutter or by cutting around a glass.

Heat the olive oil in a large frying pan and fry the tortillas in a single layer for about 1 minute each side until golden and crisp. These can be made well ahead of time.

In a small bowl, mash the avocado flesh until smooth and then mix in the spring onion, lime juice, coriander, a pinch of cayenne pepper and salt.

Season the scallops with salt and pepper and cook in the frying pan for 1 minute each side. They should be lightly golden and slightly springy to the touch. Remove from the pan and let them rest for a minute or so before cutting each scallop in half, giving you twelve discs.

To assemble the tortillas, place a teaspoon of the avocado on top of six tortilla discs, then top with a piece of scallop, repeat with the tortilla and avocado and finish with a scallop. Garnish each one with a dusting of cayenne and a slim wedge of lime. Serve straight away.

**PS . . .** Large tiger prawns can also be used on these crunchy tortilla discs.

# DUCK PÂTÉ ON BRIOCHE WITH HONEY PEARS

• MAKES 6   • 10 MINUTES

3 x 1cm-thick
  slices of brioche

1 ripe pear

a drop of olive oil

2 tablespoons runny honey

1 tablespoon orange juice

100g good-quality
  duck liver pâté

6 small sprigs of thyme,
  chervil or another herb,
  to garnish

Preheat the grill to medium.

Remove the crusts from the brioche and cut each piece into two bite-sized pieces or fingers just a little bigger than a slice of pear. Place on a baking tray and lightly grill both sides until just golden. Keep your eye on them because they will toast very quickly.

Cut the pear into six wedges, remove the core and slice away the skin. Heat a small frying pan and add a drop of oil. As soon as the oil is hot, add the pear, frying for about 1 minute on each side until golden. Drizzle over the honey and stir to coat the pear. Cook for about 30 seconds for the honey to bubble around the pears and then add the orange juice. Leave for a minute or so until the pears are totally coated in the sticky orange honey. Remove from the heat and leave to cool slightly.

Cut the pâté into thick slices just a little smaller than the brioche and place them on top of the brioche. Top each one with a slice of honey pear and a small sprig of your chosen herb. Arrange on a large plate and serve.

**PS . . .** Wedges of fig or apple are equally delicious with the pâté.

# RAREBIT TOASTS
# WITH TOMATO AND CHIVE SALAD

• MAKES 6 • 30 MINUTES, PLUS 45 MINUTES CHILLING

*for the rarebit toasts*

175g Cheddar cheese, grated

3 tablespoons milk

15g plain flour

15g fresh white breadcrumbs
(about 1 thick slice
of crustless bread)

½ teaspoon English mustard

½ teaspoon Worcestershire
sauce

1 egg yolk

3 thick slices of white bread

*for the salad*

1 large ripe tomato

sea salt and freshly ground
black pepper

1 tablespoon extra-virgin
olive oil

2 teaspoons very finely
chopped chives

1 teaspoon balsamic vinegar

To make the rarebit mixture, place the cheese and milk in a small non-stick saucepan over a medium heat to slowly melt together. Make sure the mixture doesn't boil. Add the flour, breadcrumbs, mustard and Worcestershire sauce and stir over the heat until the mixture forms a paste and leaves the sides of the pan. Remove from the heat and leave to cool.

Once cold, add the egg yolk and beat well. Chill in the fridge for about 45 minutes.

To make the salad, quarter and remove the seeds from the tomato. Finely dice the flesh and place in a small bowl. Season with salt and pepper, add the olive oil and chives and stir to combine. Keep to one side.

Preheat the grill to high.

To make the toasts, you will need a pastry cutter or glass about 5cm in diameter. Cut out six circles from the bread. Place the bread on a baking tray and toast on both sides until lightly golden. Using your hands, mould some of the rarebit to fit the shape of each piece of toast. Sit the rarebit on top and return the toast to the grill for a few minutes until golden.

Sit the rarebit toasts on to small plates and spoon the salad around the outside. Add a few drops of balsamic around the tomato and serve.

# SORBETS/PALATE CLEANSERS

*Pick the sorbet that best complements your menu.*

## CUCUMBER AND MINT SORBET

• MAKES 650ML   • 10 MINUTES, PLUS FREEZING

2 large cucumbers
100ml olive oil
1 tablespoon caster sugar
350ml vegetable stock
15g mint leaves
sea salt and freshly ground
  black pepper

Peel the cucumbers and roughly chop. Place in a food processor or blender with the olive oil, caster sugar, vegetable stock and mint leaves and season with salt and pepper. Blitz until completely smooth and then churn in an ice-cream machine or freeze according to the instructions opposite.

## LEMON, LIME AND VODKA SORBET

• MAKES 425ML   • 20 MINUTES, PLUS FREEZING

200g caster sugar
200ml fresh lemon juice,
  strained
100ml fresh lime juice
4 tablespoons lemon-flavoured
  vodka

Place the caster sugar and 300ml water in a saucepan and stir over a high heat until the sugar has dissolved. Bring to the boil and boil for 5 minutes until you have a light syrup consistency. Leave to cool and then stir in the lemon juice, lime juice and vodka. Churn in an ice-cream machine or freeze according to the instructions opposite.

## WATERMELON SORBET

• MAKES 750ML   • 20 MINUTES, PLUS FREEZING

225g caster sugar
900g watermelon flesh
75ml lime juice

Place the sugar and 125ml water in a saucepan over a high heat and stir until the sugar has dissolved. Increase the heat and boil for 1 minute. Leave to cool. Blitz the watermelon with the lime juice and strain through a sieve. You should have about 650ml juice. Mix with the sugar syrup and churn in an ice-cream machine or freeze according to the instructions opposite.

## *How to Freeze without an Ice-cream Machine*

Pour the sorbet mixture into a metal or plastic container, cover and freeze for about 1 ½ hours until the base and sides are becoming frozen. Remove and blitz in a food processor, with an electric hand whisk or energetically by hand with a balloon whisk until smooth. Refreeze, then repeat a couple more times at hourly intervals so that you end up with a smooth sorbet rather than one that is full of icy crystals.

Freshly made sorbet can be eaten straight away at the lovely 'just frozen' stage. However, if you are making it ahead of time, keep it well covered in the freezer, where it will set solid. The most important thing is to move the sorbet from the freezer into the fridge about 20 minutes before you need it, to slightly soften.

# CHEESE COURSE

## APPLE AND PEAR CRISPS

These fruity little crisps add fabulous style to any cheese board.

• SERVES 8   • 15 MINUTES, PLUS 1 HOUR IN THE OVEN

1 pear
1 apple
100g caster sugar

Preheat the oven to 160°C/fan 140°C/gas 3.

Cut the pear and apple into wafer-thin slices, ideally with a mandolin if you have one or very carefully with a knife.

Place the sugar on a plate and lightly press the apple and pear slices into it. Lay them on a couple of baking trays lined with baking paper and cook for 1 hour, turning halfway through.

Remove and carefully transfer to a wire rack until cold and crisp.

## FIG AND APRICOT CHUTNEY

Delicious with a strong Cheddar or blue cheeses.

• MAKES 375G (PLENTY FOR A COUPLE OF DINNER PARTIES)   • 40 MINUTES

125g soft dried figs, quartered
125g dried apricots, quartered
75g soft light brown sugar
100ml balsamic vinegar

Place all ingredients in a small saucepan with 100ml water over a medium heat. Stir until the sugar dissolves. Bring to the boil. Cook for 30 minutes until the figs and apricots are thick and syrupy.

Leave to cool and serve with assorted cheeses. The chutney can be stored in a sterile jar in a cool, dark place for 2 to 3 months.

**PS . . .** Why not also serve your cheese with:

Fresh figs, red and green grapes, apricots, red apples and pears.

Mini bunches of watercress or celery sticks served in shot glasses with a little water in to stop the watercress wilting.

Piles of toasted almonds, pecans and whole walnuts.

Quince jelly (membrillo), whose delicious sweet–sour flavour works perfectly with hard cheeses.

# PARMESAN OATCAKES

Repeat after me . . . 'I made these oatcakes.' Sounds good, doesn't it?

• MAKES 20   • 30 MINUTES

125g plain flour
250g fine oatmeal
2 teaspoons baking powder
½ teaspoon cayenne pepper
a pinch of salt
125g butter
75g finely grated
   Parmesan cheese

*You will also need
  a round cookie cutter
  about 5mm thick*

Preheat the oven to 180°C/fan 160°C/gas 4.

Place all of the ingredients in a food processor and blitz. Gradually add about 75ml boiling water until you have a pliable dough.

Roll out on a floured surface to about 3mm thick. Cut out the biscuits with the cutter and place on baking trays lined with greaseproof.

Bake for 12 to 15 minutes until lightly golden. Cool on the trays for a while before transferring to a wire rack to cool completely.

Store in an airtight container for up to a week.

**PS . . .** If you prefer plain oatmeal biscuits, just omit the Parmesan and cayenne and make as above.

# WALNUT AND BLUE CHEESE BISCUITS

You'll probably find people will eat your biscuits and leave the cheese selection.

• MAKES 30   • 20 MINUTES, PLUS 1 HOUR CHILLING

50g walnut halves,
  finely chopped
100g plain flour, plus extra
  for dusting
75g butter, at room
  temperature
75g Stilton cheese, crumbled
  into small pieces

Place all of the ingredients in a food processor and blend briefly until you have a firm dough.

On a floured surface and using lightly floured hands, roll into a log shape about 5cm in diameter and wrap in clingfilm. Place in the fridge for at least 1 hour to firm up.

Preheat the oven to 180°C/fan 160°C/gas 4.

The chilled log can now be cut into thin slices (2.5 to 5mm thick) and placed on baking trays lined with greaseproof. Bake for 15 to 18 minutes until lightly golden. Remove from the oven and leave to cool briefly before transferring to a wire rack to cool completely.

Store in an airtight container for up to 1 week.

**PS . . .** Pecan nuts are a nice alternative to the walnuts.

# PETITS FOURS

## CHOCOLATE CRUNCH BITES

As delicious as chocolate truffles are, they can be a fiddle to make. These wonderfully quick and simple chocolate squares are a great alternative, but be warned, they are very moreish.

• 36 SQUARES    • 20 MINUTES, PLUS AT LEAST 2 HOURS CHILLING

150g milk chocolate

150g dark chocolate

100g butter

150g golden syrup

1 tablespoon brandy
or dark rum

175g dried sultanas, raisins,
cranberries and/or cherries
(use whatever selection
you wish)

250g biscotti biscuits

50g white chocolate

*You will also need a baking
tin about 20cm square*

Place the milk chocolate, dark chocolate and butter in a bowl and gently melt in the microwave or over a pan of simmering water. Once it is smooth, stir in the golden syrup, brandy and dried fruit.

Place the biscuits in a sandwich bag and bash with a rolling pin to a coarse crumb consistency. Stir into the chocolate mixture.

Splash the baking tin with water and then line with a piece of clingfilm (the water will help the clingfilm to stick). Spoon the chocolate mixture into the tin and press into the edges with the back of a spoon.

Melt the white chocolate and drizzle over the top of the chocolate mixture in the tin. Place in the fridge for a few hours or overnight to set.

Turn out of the tin, cut into small squares and store in a cool place before serving. They will keep for days, so you don't have to eat them all at once!

**PS . . .** For a gingery kick, stir 1 ball of chopped stem ginger into the chocolate mixture with the dried fruit.

If you are making these for children, the brandy or rum doesn't have to be used. The grated zest of half an orange is a nice alternative.

# CHOCOLATE AND HAZELNUT MACAROONS

These will really add the 'wow' factor to your dinner party.

• **MAKES 16 TO 18 SMALL MACAROONS** • **45 MINUTES**

75g roasted and skinned
    hazelnuts, chopped
    or whole

175g icing sugar, sifted

2 egg whites

about 4 tablespoons chocolate
    and hazelnut spread

1 tablespoon cocoa powder

*You will also need a piping
bag with a 1cm nozzle and
a couple of baking trays
lined with parchment
paper and lightly brushed
with oil*

Preheat the oven to 170°C/fan 150°C/gas 3–4.

Place the hazelnuts in a food processor with half of the icing sugar and blitz to a fine crumb.

In a large mixing bowl, whisk the egg whites until they form stiff peaks. Add the remaining icing sugar and continue to whisk until the meringue becomes glossy. About 1 minute should be fine.

Using a large metal spoon, fold the hazelnut mixture into the meringue until combined.

Spoon into the piping bag and pipe thirty-two to thirty-six round blobs (about 2cm in diameter) on to the lined baking tray, leaving a small space between each. Let the meringues stand for about 10 minutes to allow a 'skin' to form on top and prevent them from spreading too much when cooking.

Place in the oven and cook for 15 minutes, or until they are firm but not coloured. Remove from the oven and leave to cool.

When cold, sandwich the macaroons in pairs with a smear of the chocolate and hazelnut spread.

Dust with cocoa powder and serve as they are or in mini paper muffin cases. They will keep in an airtight container for a couple of days once made.

# PEPPERMINT CREAMS

Pale green peppermint flowers, teardrops or stars, you choose. Decorate with edible glitter or dip in chocolate once made. Have fun with these.

- MAKES 50, DEPENDING ON THE SIZE OF CUTTER USED
- 30 MINUTES, PLUS 24 HOURS DRYING

1 large egg white

375–400g icing sugar, sifted, plus extra for dusting

2 teaspoons lemon juice

a few drops of peppermint flavouring

a few drops of green food colouring (optional)

Lightly whisk the egg white until it is frothy but not quite holding its shape. Gradually stir in enough of the icing sugar and lemon juice to create a pliable fondant paste.

On a surface dusted with some of the remaining icing sugar, knead in the peppermint flavouring and green food colour, if you are using it, a little at a time, until you have the flavour you're happy with and a delicate pale green colour.

Roll out to a 1cm thickness, then cut into small shapes using mini biscuit cutters or simply form into balls and flatten with your hand to give discs.

Leave for 24 hours to dry and then wrap the peppermint creams in small squares of tissue paper, twisted at the ends to look like sweets, or serve in mini paper cake cases.

# CHAPTER FOUR
# FEEDING A CROWD

There are a million reasons to have a big get-together – a surprise birthday party, New Year's Eve, a fancy-dress party, christening or house-warming, to name but a few. There's also perhaps just one excuse not to have a big get-together – the food.

What do you cook for ten to twenty people?! Well, panic no more. This chapter is full to busting with recipes that are perfect for when you're in the mood to have a party. From experience, I know there's more to a shindig than just the cooking – I mean, a new dress isn't going to buy itself. These recipes allow you to prepare ahead. They're all simple to serve, so you're not stuck in the kitchen, plating up. And they're all themed, so everything ties in.

I have concocted a New Year's Eve Moroccan-themed party, a Bonfire Night get-together, a Spanish al fresco affair and finally a family buffet. Do bear in mind how you might bring the theme out in your table decorations – it all helps to make your party a huge success.

# NEW YEAR'S EVE (MOROCCAN THEME)

*Right, it's New Year's Eve at yours this year. These recipes are very easy to prepare and simple to dish out, making it less stressful for you. They also taste delicious, combining a mixture of warming spices, herbs and fruit. Everything goes together and the theme gives you the perfect opportunity to insist everyone gets dressed up. Sounds like a great New Year's Eve party to me.*

# Menu

Fragrant Rose Champagne
  Bissara Dip

Mini Chermoula Fishcakes
  with Sweet Cucumber Relish

Chicken and Apricot Tagine
  Jewelled Couscous
    Fennel, Radish and Orange Salad

Warm Chocolate Cinnamon Torte
  with Orange Blossom Mascarpone Cream

# FRAGRANT ROSE CHAMPAGNE

A fragrant ingredient commonly used in Morocco mixed with a favourite ingredient commonly drunk on New Year's Eve.

• SERVES 6

2 tablespoons rose syrup
  (see PS . . . )
1 bottle of chilled champagne
  or sparkling wine
pink or red rose petals

Divide the rose syrup among the champagne glasses (about 1 teaspoon each) and top up with champagne or sparkling wine. Sit a rose petal on top of each and let the celebrations begin.

PS . . . You can buy beautiful pink rose syrup in bottles from supermarkets or delis, but it is easy to make your own. Boil 4 tablespoons caster sugar with 100ml water for 5 minutes until slightly syrupy. Add ¼ teaspoon rose water and 1 or 2 drops of pink or red food colouring to give a light pink colour. Leave to cool.

# BISSARA DIP

This flavoursome dip is similar to hummus, but is made using broad beans (also known as fava beans) and spices. Serve with warm flat bread or pitta bread and some nice crunchy vegetables.

• SERVES 12   • 15 MINUTES

1 tablespoon cumin seeds
3 tablespoons sesame seeds
2 x 400g tins of broad beans,
  drained
2 cloves of garlic, crushed
1 teaspoon paprika
¼ teaspoon cayenne pepper
1 teaspoon dried thyme leaves
1 teaspoon sea salt
juice of ½ large lemon
100ml olive oil

Toast the cumin seeds until they start to become fragrant and pop around the pan. Tip into a food processor. Lightly toast the sesame seeds until just golden and tip into the food processor, reserving 1 tablespoon for a garnish.

Add the remaining ingredients to the food processor and blitz to a smooth paste. If the mixture seems too thick, add a little water.

Spoon into a serving dish, drizzle over a little oil and scatter over the sesame seeds.

PS . . . Mix 400g Greek yoghurt with about 2 tablespoons harissa until smooth for an alternative spicy dip.

# MINI CHERMOULA FISHCAKES WITH SWEET CUCUMBER RELISH

There are many variations of chermoula used across Morocco, and even though it is often used as a marinade, I thought the flavours would combine well with small fishcakes to serve as a starter with a refreshing cucumber relish on the side. The relish is best made in advance and chilled. As for the fishcakes, they can be prepared and cooked ahead of time and reheated when needed.

• SERVES 12   • 1 HOUR

### for the fishcakes

2 large pinches of saffron

1kg skinless white fish fillets, such as cod, haddock or pollock

75g fresh white breadcrumbs

3 cloves of garlic, crushed

3 teaspoons ground cumin

½ teaspoon ground cinnamon

1 large red chilli, roughly chopped

finely grated zest and juice of 1 lemon

2 tablespoons runny honey

30g coriander, roughly chopped

2 eggs

sea salt and freshly ground black pepper

sunflower oil, for frying

### for the relish

1 large cucumber

2 shallots, finely chopped

2 tablespoons runny honey

grated zest of 1 orange

2 tablespoons white wine vinegar

1 small bunch of mint leaves, chopped

To prepare the fishcakes, soak the saffron in 1 tablespoon warm water for about 30 minutes.

Meanwhile, you can make the relish. Peel the cucumber, split in half and remove the seeds. Finely slice the cucumber as thinly as you can into half moons and mix together with all the remaining ingredients apart from the chopped mint. Leave in the fridge for at least 1 hour. Just before serving, stir in the chopped mint.

So, back to the fishcakes. Cut the fish into chunks and place in a food processor with the saffron and its soaking water, the breadcrumbs, garlic, cumin, cinnamon, chilli, lemon, honey, coriander, eggs and a good helping of salt and pepper. Blitz until smooth. You may need to do this in two batches, depending on the size of your processor. If you do, then try to split the quantities as evenly as possible.

Divide the mixture into thirty-six portions and, using wet hands, roll each one into a ball and flatten in the palm of your hand. Either keep covered in the fridge or cook straight away.

Heat a couple of tablespoons of oil in a large frying pan or two. Fry the fishcakes in batches for a couple of minutes each side until golden. Drain on kitchen paper while making the rest. Sit on a baking tray and, when ready to serve, heat through in a hot oven (200°C/fan 180°C/gas 6) for about 15 minutes.

Serve three fishcakes per person with a pile of Sweet Cucumber Relish on the side.

PS . . . Cooking for a crowd can get rather expensive, so you can always use tinned tuna as a cheaper alternative to fresh white fish.

# CHICKEN AND APRICOT TAGINE

In Morocco, they do a lot of belly-dancing. After you've tasted this little number, you'll understand why – it's delicious.

• SERVES 12   • ABOUT 25 MINUTES TO PREPARE AND 2½ HOURS COOKING

approx. 2kg skinless and
   boneless chicken,
      made up of a combination
      of thigh and breast
4 onions, chopped
8 cloves of garlic, crushed
100g fresh ginger,
   peeled and finely chopped
4 teaspoons ground cumin
2 teaspoons ground cinnamon
2 large pinches of saffron
2 tablespoons harissa paste
sea salt and freshly ground
   black pepper
2 litres chicken stock
700g dried apricots
8 large ripe tomatoes,
   roughly chopped
200g pitted green olives,
   halved
200g shelled unsalted
   pistachio nuts
2 bunches of coriander,
   chopped

Cut the chicken into large bite-sized chunks and split between two casserole dishes or one very large saucepan. Mix together the onion, garlic, ginger, cumin, cinnamon, saffron and harissa paste and add to the chicken. Season with salt and pepper and pour over the stock.

Bring to a simmer, cover with a lid and cook gently for about 1½ hours. Now, don't panic at this stage . . . the tagine won't look very appealing!

You can leave the tagine to cool and keep in the fridge until the next day. If you are going to do that, just gently bring back up to a simmer before continuing.

Stir the apricots, tomatoes, olives and pistachios into the tagine and simmer, uncovered, for a further 45 minutes to 1 hour, in which time the sauce will have thickened nicely and the chicken will be wonderfully tender, breaking down into smaller pieces.

Taste the tagine for seasoning, adding salt and pepper if it is needed, and stir in the coriander. The tagine is now ready to serve with the jewelled couscous (see page 228).

**PS . . .** If you are cooking for fewer people, this recipe will easily scale down.

# JEWELLED COUSCOUS

Add some bling to the couscous with the addition of sparkly pomegranate seeds.

• SERVES 12   • 15 MINUTES, PLUS 30 MINUTES IN THE OVEN

800g couscous

6 tablespoons olive oil

1.4 litres hot chicken stock

2 bunches of spring onions, finely chopped

40g butter

seeds from 2 pomegranates

2 large bunches of mint leaves, chopped

juice of 2 lemons

sea salt and freshly ground black pepper

Place the couscous in a very large bowl. Stir the olive oil into the hot stock and pour over the couscous. Stir briefly, cover with clingfilm and leave for about 5 to 10 minutes for all of the liquid to be absorbed. Fluff the couscous with a fork and leave to cool. Once cool, it can be left until the next day if necessary, to reheat when needed.

Preheat the oven to 200°C/fan 180°C/gas 6.

Place the couscous in a large ovenproof dish, mix in the spring onions and dot with butter. Cover with foil and place in the oven for about 30 minutes until heated through. Remove, stir through the pomegranate seeds, chopped mint and lemon juice and season.

PS . . . You can serve the couscous as a cold dish. Once it is cool, simply mix in the spring onions, pomegranate seeds, mint, lemon juice and seasoning. Keep at room temperature until needed.

# FENNEL, RADISH AND ORANGE SALAD

A cold side dish prepared ahead will prevent unnecessary pressure on the night.

• SERVES 12   • 20 MINUTES

4 oranges

2 medium fennel bulbs, very thinly sliced

500g radishes, cut into quarters

1 large red onion, very thinly sliced

50ml extra-virgin olive oil

sea salt and freshly ground black pepper

leaves from 1 small bunch of mint (optional)

Cut the top and bottom off each orange and sit them on a board. Following the curve of the orange, cut away the peel and pith using a sharp knife. Hold the orange over a large bowl to catch the juices and cut out the individual segments. Keep the segments to one side.

Squeeze any juice out of the remaining part of the oranges into the bowl and add the vegetables and olive oil. Season, toss together and tip into one or two large shallow serving dishes.

Arrange the oranges on top and scatter over the mint leaves just before serving, if using.

# WARM CHOCOLATE CINNAMON TORTE WITH ORANGE BLOSSOM MASCARPONE CREAM

If anyone is planning on giving up chocolate as their New Year's resolution, they might think again after a slice of this! When cooking for a crowd, it's best to make this recipe ahead of time and warm it through in the oven before serving. The delicate flavour of orange flower is a really nice addition to the sweet mascarpone cream.

• SERVES 12 • 30 MINUTES, PLUS 45 MINUTES BAKING

*for the torte*

225g butter

225g caster sugar

8 eggs, separated

225g plain chocolate, melted

225g ground almonds

½ teaspoon ground cinnamon

2 tablespoons brandy

icing sugar, to dust

*for the orange mascarpone cream*

100g icing sugar

500g mascarpone cheese

1–2 teaspoons orange flower water

orange zest, to garnish

*You will also need a 24 to 26cm loose-bottomed cake tin, greased and floured*

Preheat the oven to 180°C/fan 160°C/gas 4.

Beat together the butter and sugar until light and creamy. Gradually add the egg yolks, beating well after each one. Mix in the chocolate, ground almonds, cinnamon and brandy.

In a separate bowl, whisk the egg whites until they form soft peaks. Add one-third to the chocolate mixture to loosen and then gently fold in the rest. Pour into the prepared tin and bake for 45 minutes, until a skewer inserted into the centre of the cake comes out clean. Remove from the oven.

The cake can be served about 30 minutes after it has been cooked (this allows enough time for it to be served just warm, not hot). However, if you are making the cake ahead of time, keep it in the tin at room temperature and warm through in a low oven on about 140°C/fan 120°C/gas1–2 for 30 minutes.

To make the cream, sift the icing sugar into a bowl and beat together with the mascarpone and 1 teaspoon of the orange flower water until you have a soft, spoonable cream with a mild orange-flower flavour. If you prefer a stronger flavour, add the remaining 1 teaspoon. If the cream seems a little firm, add a tablespoon of milk to loosen.

Remove the warm cake from the tin and cut into wedges. Serve on plates with a dusting of icing sugar and finish with a spoonful of Orange Flower Mascarpone Cream, scattered with some orange zest, on the side.

# BONFIRE NIGHT

*If you have a Bonfire Night party and serve up this little lot, the firework display will be for you, not Guy Fawkes. As with all the recipes in this chapter, everything is simple to prepare and serve, leaving your guests to their own devices and you with time to enjoy yourself.*

# Menu

*Apple and Spice Vin Chaud*

*Salmon and Poppyseed Twists*

*Spicy Baked Tortilla Chips*

*Creamy Green Onion Dip*

*Roast Pumpkin and Sage Soup*
 *with Parmesan Paprika Scones*

*Creamy Sausage and Triple Mustard Casserole*

*Winter Salad Bowl*

*Chocolate Chilli Brownies*

*Toffee Apple Pies*

*Fruity Flapjacks*

# APPLE AND SPICE VIN CHAUD

On a chilly Bonfire Night, having a glass of this hot wine is a great way of warming you up from top to toe. It also gives you a cheeky glow.

• MAKES 8

1 bottle of white wine
400ml apple juice
2 sticks of cinnamon
2 star anise
100g demerara sugar
strips of rind from 1 orange

Place all of the ingredients in a saucepan over a medium heat. Stir until the sugar has dissolved and continue to heat for about 10 minutes for all of the flavours to infuse. Make sure you don't allow the wine to boil as you will lose all of the alcohol.

Serve in heatproof glasses or mugs.

**PS . . .** If you prefer, red wine can be used instead of white.

# SALMON AND POPPYSEED TWISTS

These are best served straight from the oven when the pastry is deliciously crisp, so prepare them ahead, place on a baking tray and refrigerate. It's then a quick manoeuvre from fridge to cooker just before you need them.

• MAKES ABOUT 46  • 25 MINUTES

about 150g smoked salmon,
  very thinly sliced
375g ready-rolled puff pastry
sea salt and freshly ground
  black pepper
1 egg, beaten
1 teaspoon poppy seeds

Preheat the oven to 220°C/fan 200°C/gas 8.

Lay the salmon in a single layer on top of the puff pastry and season with a twist of black pepper.

Cut the pastry in half lengthways, and then each half into 1cm thin strips. Gently twist each strip and lay them on a couple of non-stick baking trays, keeping them just slightly apart. Brush with the beaten egg and scatter over the poppy seeds and a little sea salt.

Cook in the oven for 10 to 12 minutes or until they are light golden brown.

**PS . . .** Other flavours work well with the salmon. Why not try caraway seeds, fennel seeds or sesame seeds?

# SPICY BAKED TORTILLA CHIPS

A cheaper and healthier alternative to a bag of bought tortilla chips. You can also personalize the chips with different herbs and spices to suit your taste. Serve with the Creamy Green Onion Dip.

• SERVES 8   • 15 MINUTES

6 tablespoons olive oil
½ teaspoon cayenne pepper
1 teaspoon sea salt
10 small tortilla wraps

Preheat the oven to 200°C/fan 180°C/gas 6.

Mix together the olive oil, cayenne pepper and salt and brush over both sides of the tortilla wraps. Stack them on top of one another and cut into eight triangular wedges. Place on a couple of baking trays in a single layer.

Bake in the oven for 6 to 8 minutes until golden and crispy.

Remove from the oven and serve warm or cold. Once cool, they will keep crisp for at least a week in an airtight container.

PS . . . Other flavours can be used instead of the cayenne, such as dried herbs, paprika, cumin, garam masala and all sorts of spice blends, including Cajun and Chinese five-spice.

# CREAMY GREEN ONION DIP

The perfect recipe to accompany home-made tortilla chips.

• SERVES 8   • 10 MINUTES

150ml sour cream
200g soft cream cheese
1 bunch of spring onions,
   roughly chopped
1 bunch of chives,
   roughly chopped
sea salt and freshly ground
   black pepper

Place the sour cream, cream cheese, spring onion and chives in a food processor and blend until the onions and chives are finely chopped. Season with salt and pepper and transfer to a couple of serving bowls. Keep covered in the fridge until needed.

# ROAST PUMPKIN AND SAGE SOUP
# WITH PARMESAN PAPRIKA SCONES

You can't go wrong serving a hearty soup on a chilly evening. Butternut squash can be used instead of the pumpkin.

• SERVES 8   • 45 MINUTES, PLUS 45 MINUTES COOKING

### for the soup

1 small to medium-sized
pumpkin (about 1.5kg)

2 large carrots, chopped
into 2–3cm pieces

2 large red onions, cut
into wedges

4 cloves of garlic, peeled

4 tablespoons olive oil

sea salt and freshly ground
black pepper

2 tablespoons finely
chopped sage

250ml dry white wine

1.5 litres chicken
or vegetable stock

### for the scones

350g self-raising flour,
plus extra for dusting

1 ½ teaspoons baking powder

1 teaspoon paprika,
plus extra for dusting

1 teaspoon salt

75g butter, cubed
and at room temperature

150g Parmesan cheese,
finely grated

175ml milk, plus
1 tablespoon for brushing

1 egg, beaten

Preheat the oven to 220°C/fan 200°C/gas 8.

Cut the pumpkin into wedges 2 to 3cm thick and remove any seeds. Place in one or two large roasting trays with the carrots, onion wedges and garlic. Toss in the olive oil, season and roast for about 45 minutes, turning a few times.

Meanwhile, make the scones by sifting the flour, baking powder, paprika and salt into a large mixing bowl. Rub in the butter to give you the texture of fine breadcrumbs and stir in three-quarters of the Parmesan. Gradually add the milk and beaten egg and mix until you have a soft, smooth dough, kneading lightly with your hands.

Divide the dough in two and, on a lightly floured surface, roll out two circles, about 2cm thick. Cut each piece into eight triangular wedges and sit them on a greased baking tray. Brush the tops with milk. Scatter with the remaining Parmesan and some paprika.

Bake the scones in the oven for 10 to 12 minutes or until they are golden and nicely risen. Cool slightly on a wire rack.

When the pumpkin is soft and golden, remove from the oven and, as soon as it is cool enough to handle, scoop or squeeze the flesh into a bowl. Add the carrots, onions and garlic.

Place the roasting tray over a high heat, add the sage and pour in the wine. If you are using two trays, roughly divide the wine between the two. Bring to the boil and scrape any roasted vegetables from the base of the tray. Pour in 1 litre of the stock and bring to the boil before turning off the heat.

Working in batches, blitz in a blender or food processor until smooth. Pour into a saucepan and season with salt and pepper if needed. The soup is now ready to be reheated when required, adding the extra stock if it is too thick.

Serve the hot soup in either bowls or cups with the warm, buttered scones.

**PS . . .** The scones can be made the day before needed, stored in an airtight container and warmed in the oven before serving. Alternatively they freeze really well.

Try adding different flavours with the Parmesan. Chopped walnuts or pecan nuts are great and chopped fresh herbs such as basil, rosemary, sage or thyme are also good.

# CREAMY SAUSAGE AND TRIPLE MUSTARD CASSEROLE

To make this an easy 'stand-up-and-eat' dish, the sausages are removed from their skins and rolled into balls. Obviously you can also leave them as they come if you're going to be sitting down to eat. The potatoes are cooked with the sausages, making this a whole meal in one pot. However, it's also delicious served with the Winter Salad Bowl (see page 243).

• **SERVES 8 GENEROUSLY**    • **40 MINUTES, PLUS 40 MINUTES SIMMERING**

16–24 good-quality
 pork sausages

2 tablespoons olive oil

2 large onions, thinly sliced

500g small chestnut
 mushrooms

750g potatoes, peeled
 and cut into 2cm cubes

2 medium Bramley cooking
 apples, peeled, cored and
 cut into small chunks

2 bay leaves

2 tablespoons chopped
 fresh sage

600ml vegetable
 or chicken stock

4 teaspoons Dijon mustard

2 teaspoons wholegrain
 mustard

2 teaspoons English mustard

300ml double cream

sea salt and freshly ground
 black pepper

1 bunch of flat-leaf parsley,
 chopped

Remove the sausages from their skins and roll each one into two smaller sausage shapes.

Heat the oil in one very large or two medium casserole dishes. Gently fry the sausage pieces until they are nice and golden brown all over, then remove from the pan. You may need to do this in a couple of batches due to the large number of sausages.

Add the onions to the pan and sauté until softened and becoming nicely golden. This will take a good 10 minutes.

Now, in with the mushrooms and sauté for 5 minutes. Stir in the potatoes, apple chunks, bay leaves, sage and stock. Bring to the boil and return the sausages to the pan. Reduce the heat, cover with a lid and leave to cook gently for 40 minutes, stirring a couple of times to check the sausages aren't catching on the bottom of the pan.

By now, the apple will have broken down, thickening the stock slightly. If they are soft, but still holding their shape, just mash some of them slightly with the back of a wooden spoon and stir in.

Mix the mustards into the cream and season with salt and pepper. Pour this into the casserole dish and increase the heat. Leave the lid off and simmer for about 5 to 10 minutes, or until the sauce has thickened slightly. Stir in the parsley.

Serve the casserole in bowls, preferably with a spoon to make sure you don't leave any sauce behind.

# WINTER SALAD BOWL

This recipe is made for the Creamy Sausage and Triple Mustard Casserole (see page 240).

• SERVES 8   • 15 MINUTES

100g pumpkin seeds

2 large carrots,
  coarsely grated

200g spinach leaves,
  washed and thinly sliced

1 red onion, thinly sliced

½ red cabbage, core removed
  and very thinly sliced

1 green pepper, thinly sliced

2 tablespoons red wine vinegar

6 tablespoons olive oil

½ teaspoon dried chilli flakes

1 tablespoon runny honey

sea salt and freshly ground
  back pepper

Lightly toast the pumpkin seeds in a dry frying pan.

Place the carrots, spinach, onion, cabbage, pepper and pumpkin seeds in a bowl and toss together to mix.

In a separate bowl, whisk together the red wine vinegar, olive oil, chilli and honey. Season with salt and pepper and pour over the salad. Mix well and transfer to a serving bowl.

**PS . . .** If you are preparing this ahead of time, keep the dressing separate and toss into the salad just before serving, otherwise it will become too soggy.

# CHOCOLATE CHILLI BROWNIES

The Chocolate, Cherry and Walnut Brownies were such a hit in my last book, *In the Mood for Food*, that I thought it only right to include a brownie recipe in this book. You wouldn't necessarily think of combining chocolate and chilli, but they actually work really well. The amount of chilli I am using here is just subtle enough to bring out a warmth in the gooey brownies, but certainly not enough to overpower them at all.

**• MAKES 9 TO 12 GOOD-SIZED BROWNIES   • 15 MINUTE, PLUS 25 MINUTES COOKING**

200g unsalted butter

200g dark chocolate (70% cocoa solids), chopped

3 eggs

300g granulated sugar

2 teaspoons vanilla extract

125g plain flour

½ teaspoon mild chilli powder

a pinch of salt

Preheat the oven to 180°C/fan 160°C/gas 4.

Grease and line an approximately 20 by 30cm rectangular baking tin, 3 to 4cm deep, with greaseproof or parchment paper.

Melt the butter and chocolate either in a bowl over a pan of simmering water or gently in the microwave.

With an electric hand whisk, beat together the eggs, sugar and vanilla extract until they are lovely and thick and creamy. Mix in the melted chocolate and butter. Finally stir in the flour and chilli powder.

Pour into the baking tin and cook for about 25 minutes until the top is cracking and the centre is just set. Leave to cool in the tin for about 20 minutes before removing and cutting into squares.

**PS . . .** Give the brownies a double-chocolate fix by adding 150g chopped milk or white chocolate chunks to the mixture before baking.

# TOFFEE APPLE PIES

This is my alternative to offering toffee apples, which I'm sure dentists everywhere will thank me for.

• MAKES 9   • 40 MINUTES, PLUS 20 MINUTES IN THE OVEN

200g plain flour,
  plus extra for dusting

1 teaspoon ground
  mixed spice

1 tablespoon caster sugar

sea salt

125g butter, diced, plus an
  extra 15g for the apples

2 Bramley apples
  (about 450g in weight)

4 tablespoons bought toffee
  sauce (dulce de leche)

1 egg, beaten

2 tablespoons granulated
  sugar

*You will also need
  a twelve-hole patty
  tin or bun tray and
  9cm and 6cm
  pastry cutters*

Place the flour, mixed spice, sugar and a pinch of salt in a food processor or mixing bowl and blitz or rub in the diced butter until it resembles fine breadcrumbs. Add 2 to 3 tablespoons cold water and mix until it just comes together, adding a little more water if it is needed. Knead very lightly on a floured surface to a smooth dough. Wrap in clingfilm and chill in the fridge for about 20 to 30 minutes.

Preheat the oven to 180°C/fan 160°C/gas 4.

Peel, core and cut the apples into roughly 1.5cm cubes.

Melt the remaining butter in a saucepan and add the apples along with 1 tablespoon water. Cover with a lid and cook for 10 minutes, stirring occasionally, until the apples are soft and almost puréed. Remove from the heat and cool slightly.

Roll the pastry out on a lightly floured surface and cut out nine 9cm circles and nine 6cm circles, re-rolling the pastry if necessary. Any remaining pastry can be used to cut out small shapes to top the pies with if you so wish.

Line nine holes of the patty tin with the larger circles of pastry, divide the toffee among them and then top with the apple. Dampen the edges of the pastry with water and sit the smaller circles of pastry on top. Press lightly with the back of a teaspoon to seal and pierce a hole in the top. Sit any cut shapes on top. Brush with the beaten egg and sprinkle with the granulated sugar.

Bake in the oven for 20 to 25 minutes, until the pastry is golden and crisp. Leave to cool for a few minutes in the tin before cooling further on a wire rack. Serve warm or cool.

# FRUITY FLAPJACKS

As a child, I would always make flapjacks for Bonfire Night and I've enjoyed making different versions ever since. The fruits can be swapped and changed to suit your own tastes. Apricots, peaches, apples, figs, dates, prunes, sultanas and raisins are all good choices.

• MAKES 20   • 15 MINUTES, PLUS 40 MINUTES IN THE OVEN

175g butter

175g soft brown sugar

4 tablespoons golden syrup

finely grated zest
    of ½ orange

325g porridge oats

150g dried mixed tropical
    fruits, chopped
    (such as mango, pineapple
    and papaya), cut into
    small pieces

25g desiccated coconut

Preheat the oven to 180°C/fan 160°C/gas 4.

Grease and line the base and sides of an 18cm square tin or use one with similar dimensions.

Place the butter, sugar, syrup and orange zest in a large saucepan over a medium heat and stir until the butter has melted. Remove from the heat and stir in the oats, chopped tropical fruits and desiccated coconut.

Tip into the prepared tin and bake for 40 minutes until deep golden and bubbling around the edges. The mixture will still be fairly soft in the centre, but will firm up when cooling. Leave in the tin until completely cold.

Turn the flapjacks out on to a board and cut into pieces.

PS . . . You can also put 100g chopped chocolate or nuts in the flapjacks.

# SUMMER AL FRESCO (SPANISH THEME)

*I love Spanish food so much that I've made these recipes dishes you can share. That way, you can have a bit of everything and do some al fresco mingling.* Buen provecho!

# Menu

Sherry Spritzers

Smoked Paprika and Celery Salted Almonds

Feta, Pea and Mint Tortilla

Iced Gazpacho Soup
  with Herb Croutons

Paella 'Cakes'

Chorizo, Red Pepper and Manchego Tarts

Broad Bean, Courgette and Anchovy Salad

Orange Magdalenas

Sparkling Strawberries

Crema Catalana

# SHERRY SPRITZERS

Based on the Spanish tradition of having sherry as an apéritif, this longer, refreshing version is a great way to start off your al fresco meal, along with the Smoked Paprika and Celery Salted Almonds (see page 254) and perhaps some juicy olives.

• **MAKES 8**    • **TAKES 5 MINUTES**

750ml bottle of chilled
  dry sherry
about 2.25 litres soda water
plenty of ice
lots of slices of lemon

Divide the sherry into eight tall glasses and top up with the soda (aim for about a third sherry and two-thirds soda). Add plenty of ice and a few slices of lemon.

**PS . . .** If you fancy marinating your own olives, buy a jar of black or green olives in brine. Drain well and put back in a clean jar or an airtight container. Add a couple of big strips of lemon or orange zest, ½ teaspoon dried chilli flakes, ½ teaspoon black peppercorns, 1 bay leaf and ½ teaspoon dried oregano. Top up to completely cover the olives with a good olive oil and leave to marinate for about 1 week (or longer if you can).

# SMOKED PAPRIKA
# AND CELERY SALTED ALMONDS

A very Moorish nibble to serve with an *aperitivo*.

• **MAKES 8**  • **TAKES 5 MINUTES**

2 egg whites

500g blanched almonds

2 teaspoons Spanish
   smoked paprika

1 tablespoon celery salt

2 teaspoons flaked sea salt

Preheat the oven to 200°C/fan 180°C/gas 6.

Whisk the egg white until it is light and frothy. Stir in the almonds, paprika, celery salt and sea salt.

Tip the almonds on to a lightly oiled non-stick baking tray and spread into a single layer. Roast in the oven for about 10 minutes until they are golden brown and crisp.

Leave to cool for a few minutes before tipping into a bowl, separating any that have stuck together.

**PS . . .** If you can get hold of Spanish Marcona almonds, they have a smoother, creamier texture than standard almonds, not to mention being more authentic for a Spanish theme.

# FETA, PEA AND MINT TORTILLA

Serve warm or cold. It's delicious either way.

• MAKES 8 WEDGES   • 50 MINUTES

400g new potatoes

2 tablespoons olive oil

1 large onion, sliced

2 cloves of garlic, chopped

150g frozen peas, defrosted

a small handful of mint
  leaves, roughly chopped

200g feta cheese, crumbled

6 eggs, beaten

sea salt and freshly
  ground black pepper

mint sprigs, to garnish

Cook the potatoes in boiling salted water until tender. Drain and, once they are cool enough to handle, cut into roughly 2cm chunks.

Heat the olive oil in a medium-sized non-stick frying pan (about 25cm in diameter). Cook the onion until it has softened and is just beginning to turn golden. Add the garlic and cubed potato and cook for about 3 minutes so the potatoes are heated through.

Preheat the grill to a medium heat.

Stir the peas, chopped mint and feta into the beaten eggs, season with salt and pepper, then pour the mixture into the pan. Over the lowest heat possible, cook the tortilla gently for about 10 to 15 minutes until it is almost set in the middle, carefully checking the underneath isn't burning by lifting the edge with a plastic spatula.

Place the pan under the grill for a couple of minutes to cook the top and give it a slightly golden appearance.

Slide on to a plate and serve warm or leave to cool, if you prefer. Cut into eight wedges and garnish with mint sprigs.

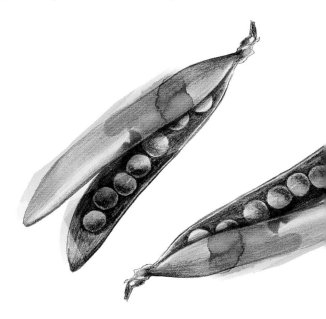

# ICED GAZPACHO SOUP WITH HERB CROUTONS

I had to include my favourite Spanish recipe of all time and the herb croutons are a lovely thing to dip into it.

• SERVES 8   • 30 MINUTES, PLUS 1 TO 2 HOURS CHILLING

1kg ripe plum tomatoes, quartered and seeds removed

1 Spanish onion, roughly chopped

¾ cucumber (about 20cm)

1 large red pepper, quartered

3 cloves of garlic, crushed

2½ thick slices of old white bread, crusts removed

750ml passata

4 tablespoons extra-virgin olive oil, plus extra for drizzling

a dash of Tabasco sauce

1½ tablespoons sherry vinegar (white wine vinegar can also be used)

sea salt and freshly ground black pepper

1 tablespoon chopped flat-leaf parsley

ice cubes, to serve

*for the herb croutons*

4 thick slices of white bread

3 tablespoons olive oil

2 teaspoons mixed dried herbs

1 teaspoon sea salt

Place the tomatoes, onion, three-quarters of the cucumber, three-quarters of the red pepper, the garlic, bread, tomato passata, olive oil, Tabasco and sherry vinegar in a blender or food processor and whizz until everything is smooth. Season with salt and pepper, then chill in the fridge for 1 to 2 hours.

Preheat the oven to 220°C/fan 200°C/gas 8.

To make the croutons, remove the crusts from the bread and cut each piece into approximately 1cm-thick strips, then cut each in half again to give you small fingers. Toss with the olive oil, herbs and salt.

Tip on to a baking tray and bake in the oven for 10 to 12 minutes until golden and crunchy, turning a couple of times throughout the cooking time. Remove from the oven and leave to cool.

When you are ready to serve the soup, remove it from the fridge. If it seems too thick, then just add a little cold water to loosen to your desired consistency.

The remaining cucumber and red pepper can now be cut into small cubes and mixed with the chopped parsley.

Ladle the soup into small bowls or cups. Add an ice cube or two to each one and spoon some of the cucumber and pepper into the middle. Drizzle a little olive oil around the outside, add a twist of pepper and serve with the herb croutons.

# PAELLA 'CAKES'

All the flavours from the wonderful Spanish paella served as individual 'cakes'. Great for making ahead and everyone will just love them.

• MAKES ABOUT 16 CAKES   • 1 HOUR, PLUS CHILLING

2 tablespoons olive oil

1 small onion, finely chopped

½ red pepper, thinly sliced

1 small skinless, boneless
  chicken breast, cut into
  tiny pieces

75g chorizo,
  cut into small cubes

200g paella rice

550ml chicken
  or vegetable stock

a pinch of saffron

½ teaspoon Spanish smoked
  paprika (normal paprika
  can also be used)

6 sun-dried tomato halves,
  finely chopped

75g frozen peas, defrosted

100g frozen cooked small
  prawns, defrosted

sea salt and freshly ground
  black pepper

1 small handful of flat-leaf
  parsley, chopped

flat-leaf parsley leaves
  and small slices of lemon,
  to garnish

Heat the olive oil in a frying pan and cook the onion until softened. Add the pepper, chicken and chorizo and cook for about 5 minutes. Stir in the rice until it's coated with the oil, then add the stock, saffron, paprika and sun-dried tomatoes. Bring to a simmer and cook for about 20 to 25 minutes or until the rice is tender and the stock has almost been absorbed.

Stir in the peas and prawns, letting them heat through for a couple of minutes.

Season with salt and pepper, stir in the chopped parsley and then remove the pan from the heat, leaving the mixture to cool.

Once the mixture is cool, firmly shape into about sixteen round, slightly flattened cakes. Put into paper cake cases and chill in the fridge until needed. Garnish the tops with parsley leaves and a slice of lemon.

**PS . . .** If you would like to make a meat-free paella, cut out the chicken and chorizo and add 250g mixed cooked seafood (fresh or a frozen bag) to the paella with the prawns.

# CHORIZO, RED PEPPER AND MANCHEGO TARTS

I love this combination of flavours and these are what can only be described as gorgeous.

• MAKES 8 INDIVIDUAL TARTS

3 tablespoons olive oil,
  plus extra for brushing
1½ red peppers, thinly sliced
1 large onion, thinly sliced
2 cloves of garlic,
  peeled and chopped
2 stalks of rosemary
sea salt and freshly ground
  black pepper
375g ready-rolled puff pastry
125g Manchego cheese, grated
100g thin slices of chorizo
caperberries,
  to serve (optional)

• 40 MINUTES, PLUS 15 MINUTES IN THE OVEN

Preheat the oven to 220°C/fan 200°C/gas 8.

Heat the olive oil in a frying pan and then gently fry the red pepper, onion, garlic and rosemary for 20 to 25 minutes until the onion and red pepper are wonderfully soft and juicy.

Season with salt and pepper, remove the rosemary stalks and leave to cool.

Unroll the pastry and either leave as a large piece or cut into eight rectangles.

Sit the pastry on a greased baking tray and score a 5mm to 1cm border around the edge with the tip of a sharp knife. Brush with a little olive oil and spoon the onion and red pepper mixture over the top, inside the border.

Scatter over half of the Manchego cheese, lay slices of chorizo, overlapping slightly, on top and then scatter with the remaining cheese.

Place in the oven and cook for about 15 minutes until the pastry around the edges is golden and the top is bubbling.

These are delicious served warm, but if you are making them for a picnic, leave to cool and pack flat.

Serve with the caperberries, if using.

# BROAD BEAN, COURGETTE AND ANCHOVY SALAD

If anyone tells you they don't like anchovies, please do encourage them to try this salad, as it uses marinated white anchovies from the deli counter. They're not at all salty like the tinned/bottled ones, but deliciously tangy, fresh and juicy. Hopefully they will convert any anchovy-hater.

• SERVES 8    • TAKES 15 TO 20 MINUTES

1.25 kg fresh broad beans,
    to give you about
    450g podded broad beans

250g baby courgettes

225g fresh marinated
    white anchovies
    (from a deli counter)

1–2 roasted red peppers,
    thinly sliced

1 bunch of flat-leaf parsley,
    chopped

1 tablespoon extra-virgin
    olive oil

sea salt and freshly ground
    black pepper

Bring a pan of salted water to the boil and cook the podded broad beans for 5 minutes. Remove with a slotted spoon and place in ice-cold water.

Slice the courgettes into rounds about 5mm thick and cook in the boiling water for 4 minutes until they are just becoming tender. Drain and leave to cool.

I know it might sound like a boring job, but the next stage is to remove the broad beans from their tough outer skin. If it is a nice day, sit outside for 5 minutes to do it. It doesn't take long and is well worth the effort, as they are lovely and tender in the salad when double-podded, not to mention the fact that they look better

Place the broad beans and courgettes in a mixing bowl with the anchovies (split into individual fillets if they aren't already), red peppers, chopped parsley and olive oil. Season with salt and pepper and mix together, then transfer to a serving bowl to serve.

**PS . . .** You can use frozen broad beans for this recipe. Just bear in mind that they won't need to be boiled, just defrosted and removed from their skin. If you are using baby broad beans, the double-podding might not be necessary.

# ORANGE MAGDALENAS

Traditionally these moist little cakes are made with olive oil and flavoured with lemon zest, but I think the orange flavour goes really well too, especially with the Sparkling Strawberries. They will last a couple of days in an airtight container.

• MAKES 16   • 15 MINUTES, PLUS 20 MINUTES IN THE OVEN

115g plain flour
50g caster sugar
finely grated rind of 1 orange
100ml olive oil
3 eggs, separated
2 tablespoons milk
icing sugar, to dust

*You will also need one to two patty tins or bun trays lined with paper cake cases*

Preheat the oven to 180°C/fan 160°C/gas 4.

Mix together the flour, sugar, orange rind, olive oil, egg yolks and milk.

Whisk the egg whites until they are stiff. Stir a quarter of the whites into the cake mixture to loosen, then fold in the rest of the whites with a large metal spoon.

Spoon the cake mixture into the cake cases so they are about two-thirds full. You might need to keep some mixture back if you are using just one patty tin.

Bake for 20 minutes until golden and just firm to the touch. As they cook, it is usual for the cakes to peak in the middle, crack slightly and then flatten back down when cooling.

Remove and leave to cool for a couple of minutes in the tin/s. Cool on a wire rack and then dust heavily with icing sugar before serving.

# SPARKLING STRAWBERRIES

Delicious to serve with the Orange Magdalenas.

• SERVES 8 TO 12   • 5 MINUTES

500g strawberries
icing sugar, for dusting
½ bottle of chilled pink cava

Cut the strawberries in half or quarters if they are particularly large.

Place in a serving bowl or individual champagne flutes or wine glasses. Dust heavily with icing sugar. The amount you use will depend on the sweetness of the strawberries, but don't be shy with it.

Pour over the cava and leave for about 30 minutes before serving.

# CREMA CATALANA

This creamy Spanish dessert is very similar to the French crème brûlée with its rich creamy custard and crunchy caramel top. It is, however, a lot easier to prepare and serve, especially for a large group of people.

• SERVES 8  • 25 MINUTES, PLUS A COUPLE OF HOURS CHILLING

6 egg yolks

250g caster sugar

3 tablespoons cornflour

750ml milk

1 cinnamon stick

2–3 pieces of peeled lemon zest

1 teaspoon vanilla extract

*You will also need eight approximately 150ml capacity ramekins or small dishes*

Beat together the egg yolks and just 150g of the caster sugar until wonderfully light, pale and fluffy.

Mix the cornflour with a couple of tablespoons of the milk and keep to one side.

Pour the remaining milk into a saucepan, add the cinnamon and lemon zest and gently bring to the boil. Remove from the heat and stir into the egg and sugar mixture. Add the vanilla extract and cornflour mixture, then return to the saucepan. Place over a gentle heat and stir continuously until the mixture starts to bubble.

Pour into the dishes, keeping back the cinnamon and lemon zest, smooth the tops over and leave to cool before putting in the fridge to chill. They can be stored in the fridge the day before you want them if need be.

To prepare the caramel topping, put the remaining 100g of caster sugar in a saucepan with 100ml water. Place over a gentle heat and stir until the sugar has dissolved. Increase the heat and leave the syrup to boil rapidly until it is a rich golden colour. Remove from the heat and pour immediately on to an oiled baking tray. Leave to cool and, as it cools, it will set completely solid. This can be made well ahead of time and stored in a cool place.

When you are ready to serve, snap the caramel into small pieces/shards or bash in a sandwich bag with a rolling pin for even smaller bits and scatter over the top of each dessert. Serve straight away.

# FAMILY BUFFET

*This is perfect for any family occasion or celebration. If your guests end up standing, perched on a garden wall or stuck in a corner with your great-uncle, they'll at least find something here that they can tuck in to.*

# Menu

*Pistachio and Orange Roast Ham*

*Salmon, Prawn and Potato Salad
 with Creamy Dill Dressing*

*Goat's Cheese, Leek and Baby Tomato Tart*

*Tangy Quinoa and Herb Salad
 with Mango*

*Chicken and Pancetta Pasta Salad
 with Tarragon and Lemon Pesto*

*Green and White Bean Salad*

*Black Forest Mess*

*Classic Banoffee Pie*

*Favourite Fruit Tart*

# PISTACHIO AND ORANGE ROAST HAM

It wouldn't be a proper buffet without a piece of ham on the table.

• SERVES 12 EASILY   • 20 MINUTES, PLUS 2½ HOURS BOILING AND 30 MINUTES ROASTING

approx. 3kg piece of gammon

stock ingredients:
  1 small onion, 1 carrot,
  1 potato, 2 sticks of celery,
  4 cloves of peeled garlic,
  1 bay leaf and 1 teaspoon
  black peppercorns

75g shelled, unsalted
  pistachio nuts

2 tablespoons Dijon mustard

75g demerara sugar

grated zest of 1 orange

Place the gammon in a large saucepan and cover with cold water. Bring to the boil and then drain. Rinse well, return to the pan and refill with cold water.

Peel the onion, carrot and potato and cut in half along with the celery. Add to the pan with the garlic, bay leaf and peppercorns. Cover with a lid and bring to the boil. Reduce the heat so the water is simmering, cover loosely with a lid and cook for 2½ hours. Check the water isn't boiling away too much. You can top up with a little hot water a couple of times if it is.

Once the ham has had its cooking time, preheat the oven to 200°C/fan 180°C/gas 6.

Lift the ham out of the pan, keeping the cooking liquid. As soon as it is cool enough to handle, remove the skin (it should peel or slice away quite easily), making sure you leave a thin layer of fat behind. Score the fat in a criss-cross pattern with a sharp knife.

Chop the pistachios very finely and then mix together with the mustard, sugar and orange zest and spread over the scored fat. Sit in a roasting tray and pour a few millimetres of the cooking liquid into the base to prevent any of the crust that might drip into the tray from burning in the bottom.

Place in the oven for 30 minutes, until the glaze is golden and bubbling.

The ham can now be left to rest for about 20 minutes if you want to serve it hot or to cool completely, after which it can be kept in the fridge for a few days.

**PS . . .** The cooking liquid can be used as delicious-tasting stock for making gravies, soups and sauces.

# SALMON, PRAWN AND POTATO SALAD WITH CREAMY DILL DRESSING

This recipe will take a bit of pre-planning because you may have to order the fish and then you'll need to cook it the day before, to allow time for it to cool down. That aside, it is a very simple recipe and the quantities can be scaled down for fewer people.

• SERVES 12   • 45 MINUTES, PLUS 2½ HOURS TO COOK THE SALMON

approx. 2kg whole salmon, gutted and scaled

50g butter

1 small onion, sliced

4 bay leaves

4 sprigs of dill

4 slices of lemon

sea salt and freshly ground black pepper

400g raw peeled tiger prawns

750g waxy new potatoes, such as Charlotte

2 large sprigs of mint

2 bunches of spring onions, thinly sliced on an angle

100g watercress sprigs or pea shoots

*for the dressing*

250ml sour cream

juice of 1 lemon

1 bunch of dill, finely chopped

4 tablespoons cooking juices from the fish (or cold fish stock)

75g gherkins, finely chopped

2 tablespoons Dijon mustard

sea salt and freshly ground black pepper

Preheat the oven to 150°C/fan 130°C/gas 2.

Place the fish in the middle of a large double piece of foil that has been buttered generously with most of the 50g of butter. Place the remaining butter in the fish cavity with the sliced onion, bay leaves, dill sprigs and sliced lemon and season both the cavity and all over the fish with salt and pepper. Loosely wrap the foil over the salmon and tightly seal the parcel. Place on a baking tray in the oven. If the fish is too long, just curl up the tail so it fits. Cook slowly for 2 hours.

Carefully open the foil and scatter the prawns around the salmon. Reseal and return to the oven for a further 30 minutes. Remove from the oven and leave to cool completely, still sealed.

Once the fish is cool, open the parcel, peel away the skin (which should happen really easily) and break the flesh into thick flakes, removing any bones. This is quite a slow job, but try not to rush it because it is really nice to keep some large flakes to the salmon. Keep the salmon to one side. As for the prawns, place them in a bowl and cover with the fish juices to keep moist until needed.

Cook the potatoes in boiling salted water with the sprigs of mint until tender. Drain and leave to cool. Slice into halves or quarters, depending on their size.

To make the dressing, mix everything together and season. Stir half into the potatoes with the spring onions.

Scatter the watercress or pea shoots on a large serving platter and arrange the potatoes, salmon and prawns on top. Spoon over some of the remaining dressing and place the rest in a bowl to serve separately.

Serve straight away or keep covered in the fridge for up to 2 hours.

# GOAT'S CHEESE, LEEK AND BABY TOMATO TART

If you are making this contemporary version of a quiche in advance, cover with tin foil and keep at room temperature.

• SERVES 12  • 30 MINUTES, PLUS 20 MINUTES RESTING AND 30–40 MINUTES COOKING

500g puff pastry

2 tablespoons olive oil

2 medium leeks,
   thinly sliced

2 cloves of garlic, crushed

350g soft, mild goat's cheese

3 large eggs, lightly beaten

150ml single cream

2 tablespoons fresh
   thyme leaves

sea salt and freshly ground
   black pepper

150g baby plum
   or cherry tomatoes, halved

50g Parmesan cheese, grated

*You will also need a
   tart ring or loose-bottomed
   tart/flan tin approximately
   25cm x 3cm, lightly
   greased and placed on
   a baking tray*

Preheat the oven to 200°C/fan 180°C/gas 6.

Roll the pastry out on a lightly floured surface and cut to a circle a little bigger that the tart ring. Line the ring with the pastry, lightly pressing it into the base and sides and easing any overhanging pastry back down so it sits about 5mm above the top. This will allow for shrinkage when cooking. Prick the base several times with a fork. The beauty of using puff pastry is that it will still look good even if it seems uneven when cooked, so don't worry about it too much.

Place in the fridge for about 20 minutes to rest.

When it has rested, line the pastry case with greaseproof paper and fill with baking beans or rice. Place in the oven for 15 minutes, then remove the paper and beans and return to the oven for a further 5 minutes.

While the pastry is cooking, heat the olive oil in a frying pan and lightly sauté the sliced leeks and garlic until the leeks are softened but not coloured. Cool slightly.

Reduce the oven to 180°C/fan 160°C/gas 4.

Mix together the goat's cheese, eggs, cream, thyme and seasoning and beat until smooth. This can be done really quickly in a food processor. Mix into the leeks and pour into the pastry case. Arrange the tomatoes over the top, cut-side up, and scatter over the Parmesan cheese.

Bake for 30 to 40 minutes until the cheese filling has set and the Parmesan is becoming golden. Remove from the oven and leave in the ring for about 10 minutes before removing to serve, either warm or cold.

# TANGY QUINOA AND HERB SALAD WITH MANGO

This is a modern and very healthy alternative to a rice salad or tabbouleh. If you want to make this into a more substantial recipe, crumbled feta cheese is really nice, especially if you have a few vegetarians at your party.

• SERVES 12   • 20 MINUTES

approximately 2 litres
    chicken stock

500g quinoa

1 fairly ripe mango,
    peeled and finely chopped

1 cucumber, peeled,
    deseeded and finely diced

1 red onion, finely chopped

1 bunch of flat-leaf parsley,
    chopped

1 bunch of mint leaves,
    finely chopped

finely grated zest
    and juice of 1 lemon

100ml extra-virgin olive oil

50ml white wine vinegar

sea salt and freshly ground
    black pepper

Bring the stock to the boil in a large saucepan. Stir in the quinoa, return to the boil and simmer, uncovered, for about 10 to 12 minutes. It may need a little longer, but you will know it is cooked when rings around the centre of the grains begin to detach themselves.

Drain the quinoa really well, shaking in the sieve to separate all the grains, and then tip into a large mixing bowl and leave to cool.

Add all of the remaining ingredients to the quinoa and mix well.

The salad can be served straight away, but will benefit from sitting a while, overnight even, for the flavours to develop. Stir before serving.

# CHICKEN AND PANCETTA PASTA SALAD WITH TARRAGON AND LEMON PESTO

This is fine to make the day before it is needed. In fact, the flavours are even better the next day.

• SERVES 12 • MINUTES, PLUS 1 HOUR MARINATING

4 skinless, boneless
   chicken breasts

grated zest and juice of
   1 lemon

1 clove of garlic, sliced

3 tablespoons olive oil

sea salt and freshly ground
   black pepper

750g penne pasta

200g pancetta, diced

100g rocket or watercress
   sprigs

*for the pesto*

75g pine nuts

75g Parmesan cheese, grated

20g tarragon leaves, roughly
   chopped

grated zest of 1 lemon, plus
   the juice of ½ lemon

1 clove of garlic, chopped

100ml extra-virgin olive oil
   (a nice fruity one)

sea salt and freshly ground
   black pepper

Start off by placing the chicken in a dish and adding the lemon zest and juice, garlic, 1 tablespoon of the olive oil and seasoning with salt and pepper. Leave to marinate for an hour or so.

Meanwhile, cook the pasta until al dente. Drain, refresh under cold water and toss in 1 tablespoon of the olive oil to prevent it from sticking. Keep to one side.

Heat a large frying pan and add the remaining tablespoon of olive oil. Gently fry the pancetta until it is lightly golden and starting to go crispy. Remove with a slotted spoon and drain on kitchen paper.

Lift the chicken from the marinade and then fry in the pancetta pan for about 4 minutes on each side or until it is just cooked through. Leave to cool, then slice into bite-sized pieces and keep covered.

The final thing that has to be prepared is the pesto. Very lightly toast the pine nuts in a dry frying pan and then, when cool, place with everything else in a small food processor and whizz to a smooth consistency. Season with salt and pepper.

To put the salad together, toss the cooked pasta, pancetta, cooked chicken, pesto and rocket or watercress together and transfer to a large bowl. If you are not serving the salad within 30 minutes, leave out the rocket or watercress and stir in at the last minute.

**PS . . .** For a meat-free pasta salad, the chicken and pancetta can be replaced with steamed or sautéed sliced courgettes, steamed sugar snap peas, peas and/or broad beans. A couple of handfuls of sunblush tomatoes are a great addition to the salad too.

# GREEN AND WHITE BEAN SALAD

This salad actually benefits from being made a few hours ahead of time, allowing the beans to really take on the flavours from the dressing.

• SERVES 12  • 20 MINUTES

500g green beans,
  trimmed and cut in half

100g pine nuts

400g tin of cannellini beans

400g tin of flageolet beans

400g tin of haricot beans

1 red onion, very thinly sliced

*for the dressing*

2 cloves of garlic, crushed

2 large handfuls of flat-leaf
  parsley leaves

1 handful of basil leaves

2 tablespoons capers

1 tablespoon Dijon mustard

3 tablespoons red wine vinegar

8 tablespoons extra-virgin
  olive oil (a nice fruity one)

sea salt and freshly ground
  black pepper

Cook the green beans in boiling salted water for a few minutes until they are tender. Drain and refresh under the cold tap. Pat dry and place in a large bowl.

Toast the pine nuts in a dry frying pan.

Drain the tinned beans and add to the green beans, along with the red onion and pine nuts.

To make a dressing, place the garlic, parsley, basil, capers, mustard, red wine vinegar and olive oil in a food processor and blend until the herbs are fairly finely chopped.

Pour the dressing over the beans, season with salt and pepper and spoon into a serving dish.

# BLACK FOREST MESS

This recipe started off as Black Forest pavlovas – individual chocolate meringue nests with cherry kirsch cream and cherry compote – which I was planning on making for my son's christening. They went wrong! I was very distracted while making the meringue, with all our friends arriving for the weekend, resulting in the meringues not holding their shape. The next day, after realizing they wouldn't look very good as individual desserts, I crumbled them up and created a chocolate cherry version of an Eton Mess. It was a real hit and a blessing in disguise as they took no time at all to finish off. So I decided to keep the recipe for this book.

• SERVES 8    • TAKES 30 MINUTES, PLUS 1 ½ HOURS FOR COOKING THE MERINGUES

6 egg whites

350g caster sugar

1 teaspoon white wine vinegar

25g cocoa powder

1 tablespoon cornflour

600ml double cream

3 tablespoons kirsch
   (cherry liqueur)

about 400g cherry compote
   (see PS . . . )

2 tablespoons
   grated chocolate

Preheat the oven to 140°C/fan 120°C/gas 1–2.

To make the meringues, whisk the egg whites until they form stiff peaks. Gradually add the caster sugar and continue to whisk for a few minutes before adding the vinegar and sifting in the cocoa powder and cornflour. Whisk until you have a firm, glossy and super-creamy consistency, a bit like shaving foam.

Place a piece of parchment paper on a baking tray and lightly brush with a little sunflower or vegetable oil. Drop about eight to ten large spoonfuls of the meringue on to the paper, leaving a small space between each for them to spread slightly.

Bake for 1 ½ hours until the outsides are crispy, but not becoming golden. Turn off the oven and leave to cool with the door slightly open. When the meringues have cooled, carefully peel away from the paper. The meringues can be made a day or two in advance and kept in an airtight container.

To put the dessert together, whip the cream in a large bowl until it just starts to thicken. Add the kirsch and continue to whisk until soft peaks form. Break the meringues into pieces and gently fold into the cream with the cherry compote.

Spoon into a large serving bowl or individual bowls and scatter with some of the grated chocolate.

PS . . . If you can't get hold of cherry compote, a combination of black cherry jam and tinned and drained black cherries or frozen cherries works really well.

# CLASSIC BANOFFEE PIE

This is a bit of a cheat recipe really, because there is very little to do, but it looks divine and will no doubt be the first pudding to go.

• SERVES 8 • 20 MINUTES, PLUS CHILLING FOR AT LEAST 1 ½ HOURS

125g butter

300g digestive biscuits, finely crushed

about 400g bought toffee sauce (dulce de leche)

2 large bananas

275ml double cream

2 tablespoons chocolate shavings

*You will also need a 22cm loose-bottomed deep flan tin, lightly greased*

To make the base, melt the butter in a large saucepan and stir in the crushed biscuits. Press into the base and partly up the sides of the tin. Place in the fridge to chill for about 30 minutes or so.

Spread the toffee sauce over the biscuit base and chill for at least 1 hour (overnight is fine).

When you are ready to serve, peel and slice the bananas and lay them over the toffee.

Whip the cream until it forms soft peaks and spoon over the top of the bananas. Scatter over the chocolate, remove from the tin and serve.

# FAVOURITE FRUIT TART

I have very fond memories of a delicious, yet extremely simple, apricot tart from when I stayed with a French family as a teenager. It consisted of sweet pastry with crisp edges and a soft inside packed full of juicy apricots. It makes a great recipe for a family buffet and you can choose all sorts of fruits. Peaches, nectarines, pears, apples, plums and, of course, apricots are all great. It's best cooked the day it's needed. However, the pastry case can be lined and kept in the fridge for up to 2 days before using.

• SERVES 8 • 25 MINUTES, PLUS 30 MINUTES RESTING AND 1 ½ HOURS COOKING

225g plain flour,
   plus extra for dusting
150g butter
75g caster sugar
1 egg plus 1 egg yolk, beaten
750g–1kg of your chosen fruit
icing sugar, to dust
double cream, to serve

*You will also need a 23cm
   to 24cm plain or fluted
   shallow tart/flan tin*

To make the pastry, place the flour, butter and sugar in a food processor or mixing bowl and blitz briefly or rub in the butter until it resembles breadcrumbs. Slowly add the egg a little at a time until the pastry binds together. Knead very lightly on a floured surface to a smooth dough.

Roll out the pastry and line the tart tin, trimming any excess pastry. Place in the fridge for 30 minutes (or up to 2 days) covered loosely with clingfilm.

Preheat the oven to 160°C/fan 140°C/gas 2–3. Place a baking tray in the oven to heat up.

To prepare the fruit, slice in half (apricots or plums), cut into thick wedges (peaches and nectarines) or thinly slice (apples or pears), removing any stones, pips or cores as you go.

Working from the outside in, really pack the fruit into the pasty case (it does shrink when cooking) and dust with a generous amount of icing sugar.

Place in the oven on top of the hot baking tray. Cook for 30 minutes before reducing the oven temperature to 140°C/fan 120°C/gas 1–2 and cooking for a further 45 minutes to 1 hour, or until the fruits are becoming golden on top.

Cool in the tin slightly before carefully removing and dusting again with icing sugar. Serve warm or at room temperature.

# INDEX

# A MASSIVE THANK YOU TO:

*all my family and friends (for being the chief tasters), Lindsey Evans at Penguin (for all her support throughout the book writing process), Sarah Fraser (for another beautifully designed book), Sarah Hulbert, Kay Halsey, the sales team and publicity department and anyone else at Penguin that I've not mentioned who has helped get this book on to the shelves, Gareth Morgans (for the beautiful photography – it was great fun and a real pleasure), Wei Tang (for her creative prop styling), my fantastic sister Millie and Emily (for all their hard work on the shoot, getting all of the food prepared and keeping the kitchen wonderfully organized while I caused chaos), Susie Barrie (for the delicious wine matches for the different menus throughout the book – cheers, Susie), Camilla Stoddart (for giving me the chance of a second book) and finally, and that's not intentional, my fab agent Borra Garson and her team at DML.*